Hinduism: A Very Short Introduction

'strongly recommended both for its exemplification of the finest
contemporary thinking in this area and its attention to central matters
and issues'
Peter Doble, *Theological Book Review*

'a very accessible overview. The rich diversity within Hinduism is
celebrated and the difficult questions are not avoided'
Inter-Faith Issues

'accessible and enjoyable'
Arti Kachhia, *ISKON Communications Journal*

'very readable and certainly most helpful, with a new and original
perspective conveyed in a succinct introductory style'
Ursula King, University of Bristol

VERY SHORT INTRODUCTIONS are for anyone wanting a stimulating
and accessible way in to a new subject. They are written by experts, and have
been published in more than 25 languages worldwide.

The series began in 1995, and now represents a wide variety of topics
in history, philosophy, religion, science, and the humanities. Over the next
few years it will grow to a library of around 200 volumes – a Very Short
Introduction to everything from ancient Egypt and Indian philosophy to
conceptual art and cosmology.

Very Short Introductions available now:

Available soon:

THE TUDORS   John Guy
TWENTIETH-CENTURY
   BRITAIN   Kenneth O. Morgan
WITTGENSTEIN   A. C. Grayling
WORLD MUSIC   Philip Bohlman
AFRICAN HISTORY
   John Parker and Richard Rathbone
ANCIENT EGYPT   Ian Shaw
THE BRAIN   Michael O'Shea
BUDDHIST ETHICS
   Damien Keown
CHAOS   Leonard Smith
CHRISTIANITY   Linda Woodhead
CITIZENSHIP   Richard Bellamy
CLASSICAL ARCHITECTURE
   Robert Tavernor
CLONING   Arlene Judith Klotzko
CONTEMPORARY ART
   Julian Stallabrass
THE CRUSADES
   Christopher Tyerman
DERRIDA   Simon Glendinning
DESIGN   John Heskett
DINOSAURS   David Norman
DREAMING   J. Allan Hobson
ECONOMICS   Partha Dasgupta
THE END OF THE WORLD
   Bill McGuire
EXISTENTIALISM   Thomas Flynn
THE FIRST WORLD WAR
   Michael Howard
FREE WILL   Thomas Pink

FUNDAMENTALISM
   Malise Ruthven
HABERMAS   Gordon Finlayson
HIEROGLYPHS
   Penelope Wilson
HIROSHIMA   B. R. Tomlinson
HUMAN EVOLUTION
   Bernard Wood
INTERNATIONAL RELATIONS
   Paul Wilkinson
JAZZ   Brian Morton
MANDELA   Tom Lodge
MEDICAL ETHICS
   Tony Hope
THE MIND   Martin Davies
MYTH   Robert Segal
NATIONALISM   Steven Grosby
PERCEPTION   Richard Gregory
PHILOSOPHY OF RELIGION
   Jack Copeland and Diane Proudfoot
PHOTOGRAPHY   Steve Edwards
THE RAJ   Denis Judd
THE RENAISSANCE
   Jerry Brotton
RENAISSANCE ART
   Geraldine Johnson
SARTRE   Christina Howells
THE SPANISH CIVIL WAR
   Helen Graham
TRAGEDY   Adrian Poole
THE TWENTIETH CENTURY
   Martin Conway

For more information visit our web site
www.oup.co.uk/vsi

Kim Knott

HINDUISM

A Very Short Introduction

OXFORD
UNIVERSITY PRESS

OXFORD

UNIVERSITY PRESS

Great Clarendon Street, Oxford OX2 6DP

Oxford University Press is a department of the University of Oxford.
It furthers the University's objective of excellence in research, scholarship,
and education by publishing worldwide in

Oxford New York

Auckland Bangkok Buenos Aires Cape Town Chennai
Dar es Salaam Delhi Hong Kong Istanbul Karachi Kolkata
Kuala Lumpur Madrid Melbourne Mexico City Mumbai Nairobi
São Paulo Shanghai Taipei Tokyo Toronto

Oxford is a registered trade mark of Oxford University Press
in the UK and in certain other countries

Published in the United States
by Oxford University Press Inc., New York

© Kim Knott 1998

The moral rights of the author have been asserted
Database right Oxford University Press (maker)

First published 1998
Reissued 2000

British Library Cataloguing in Publication Data

Data available

Library of Congress Cataloging in Publication Data

Knott, Kim.
Hinduism.
(Very short introduction)
Includes bibliographical references and index.
1. Hinduism.   I. Series.
BL1202.K564 1998   294.5—dc21   98–10944

ISBN 978-0-19-285387-5

19 20

Typeset by RefineCatch Ltd, Bungay, Suffolk
Printed in Great Britain by
Ashford Colour Press Ltd, Gosport, Hants

Preface

Hindu gods and goddesses are everywhere in India, hidden within gorgeous temples and small wayside shrines, depicted in intricate stone carvings, looking out benevolently from advertisements, calendar prints, and film posters, and captured on market stalls and in shop windows in jewellery and small sculptures. They are woven into the fabric of life in Indian villages and cities, and are now also to be found in Hindu communities from the Caribbean to North America and the UK, from South Africa to Thailand. They are much loved by all. The many places in which they appear and the multitude of forms they take indicate the diversity and richness of Hindu culture.

But Hinduism extends beyond culture into other spheres – into the social structure and social life of Hindus, ethical issues, and the politics of equality and nationalism. Contemporary Hinduism and its traditional stories, teachings, and rituals affect so many aspects of the lives of Indians in and beyond the sub-continent that we begin to wonder how to define it. Is it appropriate to call it 'a religion'? Is it like Christianity or Islam? In what ways does it differ? Does it, in fact, challenge our notions of what a religion is?

This introduction to Hinduism takes us into a consideration of these issues. It begins by raising the question of how different starting points influence the way we perceive and understand Hinduism. How far do the motives and conclusions of devotees and scholars differ, for example? In the following chapters we learn about the importance to Hindus of the traditions contained in their scriptures, of their initial revelation and subsequent transmission from generation to generation by priests, gurus, and storytellers.

One of the important questions considered and handed down by Hindus over many centuries has been 'Who am I?' or, to put it another way, 'What is the self?' Philosophers have discussed the nature of the self, its relationship to God and the world, whether it continues after death, and how it is affected by our actions. These are still valid issues. In Chapter 3, we look at how they were debated in earlier times and at their contemporary relevance.

In the next two chapters, we are introduced to a variety of Hindu gods and goddesses, the stories told about them, the way they are depicted in sculpture and pictures, and the worship that is offered to them. Rama, Sita, Durga, Ganesha, Vishnu, Shiva, and Krishna are described. But we also consider how Hindus understand the divine. Do they worship many gods at once, or are these all just forms of a single divine being? Is it possible that there is some truth in both of these ideas?

In the seventeenth and eighteenth centuries, when Europeans first came into contact with Hindu ideas about the divine, and with Hindu rituals and social life, they were puzzled and shocked. They saw it all through the lens of their own religion and culture, and they compared it with their own experience, often drawing unfavourable conclusions. In Chapter 6, we consider the relationship of European and American outsiders to Hinduism, and reflect upon the impact of British colonialism on religious developments in India in recent centuries. Early on, Hindu reformers and British administrators in India began to call for equality and social change, particularly for women and those people stigmatized as 'untouchable' by higher-caste Hindus. In Chapter 7, we turn to the views of women and untouchables, *dalits* as they are now known, and consider their place within Hinduism.

It is not only these two large minorities which raise challenging questions about who is a Hindu. Those Indians who contravened an early Hindu teaching and crossed 'the black waters' stepped outside the sacred territory of India. Yet, in Indian communities worldwide, temples have been established, Hindu movements have spread, and Hindu ideas and rituals have been transmitted. Aspects of Hinduism have even been taught to interested non-Hindus, thus raising the question of whether Hinduism remains a religion solely for those born into Indian families and Hindu castes, or whether it has now become a missionary religion.

This and other questions about the identity of Hinduism are discussed in the final chapter. Is it one religion or many different religions each defined by region, caste, and sect? Is it a religion at all? Does it make us think about the subject of religion in new ways? Although it is quite impossible to answer all these questions satisfactorily, by discussing them we are able to appreciate the extraordinary complexity, diversity, and dynamism of all that we call Hinduism.

Acknowledgements

I would like to thank everyone who has helped me write this book. I am indebted to all those who have taught me about Hinduism, to my teachers, Hindu friends, and colleagues. Detailed footnoting has not been appropriate, and in its absence I express my gratitude to those whose work has helped me to describe and explain Hinduism. A particular 'Thank you' goes to my students, to those who took my course in 1997 when I tried out my ideas, to the postgraduates who inspired me, and to all those over the years who showed an interest in Hinduism and encouraged me to make it accessible to them. Without this practice, I could not have attempted this task.

I would also like to thank those who assisted with the production of the manuscript and its publication: the publisher's readers, particularly Julia Leslie, for their constructive advice and informed comments, Tamsin Shelton for her speed and precision, and George Miller and Shelley Cox at Oxford University Press for support and guidance throughout the process. I also benefited immensely from the kindness, imagination, and attention to detail of family and friends who read the draft manuscript: special thanks to my mother, Kay Knott, my husband, John Murdoch, Ursula King, Eleanor Nesbitt, Ram Krishan Prashar, and Bob Jackson. I had helpful conversations with other friends and postgraduates in the formative stages, especially Nilaben Pancholi, Sewa Singh Kalsi, Gavin Flood, Jackie Hurst, Subash Sharma, Bob Exon,

Preeti Tyagi, and Daphne Green. I would also like to express my appreciation for the support given me by colleagues at the University of Leeds, especially in the Department of Theology and Religious Studies. They helped me to remain enthusiastic about writing an introductory book at a time when research monographs and articles were assessed to be of higher academic value. A period of study leave enabled me to complete the project on time.

I have immensely enjoyed writing this book and thank those at OUP for giving me the opportunity. I have always admired those who could make difficult subjects interesting and approachable without diluting their complexity or distorting their meaning. To be given this as a goal was an inviting challenge that I could not resist. Whether I have been able to achieve this for Hinduism will best be judged by those who give time to reading what follows.

Final love and thanks go to my daughter, Anita, who has provided me with joyful and welcome breaks after each day's work. Without 'the spaces in-between', this would have been a lesser book.

Contents

List of Illustrations

List of Maps

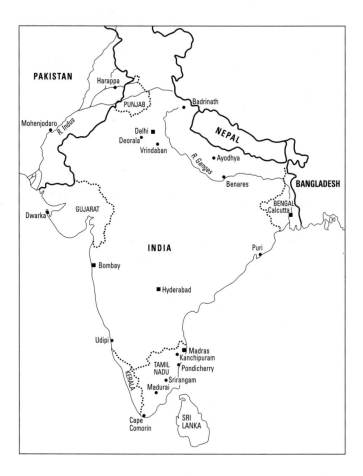

Map 1. The Indian Subcontinent, with religious sites

Chapter 1
The Scholar and the Devotee

If you go into a library or bookshop with the intention of finding out about Hinduism, to which section do you go? To 'Sociology' for books on the social system of the Hindus? To 'Art and Architecture' to learn about the fabulous temples, carvings, and paintings in which Hindu mythology is depicted? To 'Languages' for books on Sanskrit and other Indian languages? To 'Anthropology' for information about village India, its society and culture? Although you might well find useful sources in all these locations, you would probably go first to the 'Religion' section, because in Western countries Hinduism is considered to be a religious system much like Judaism, Christianity, Islam, and Buddhism.

One of the key issues to be considered in this short introduction is the extent to which this is true. Is Hinduism a religion like others, and what are the principal characteristics which define it? In each of the following chapters, as well as discussing a particular theme, I will raise the question of what that theme may tell us about the nature of Hinduism, the religious system of the Hindus. For example, in the next chapter the centrality for Hinduism of a collection of religious texts known as *Veda* and the culture of the brahmins, the caste of ritual specialists, will be discussed.* Then, in the penultimate chapter, I will consider to what

---

* There is a glossary at the back of the book in which the meanings of Hindu terms are explained.

extent Hinduism can flourish outside India and whether or not someone can choose to be a Hindu. Is Hinduism a religion for all or only for those born into Hindu families?

In the final chapter I will return to the subject of the nature and definition of Hinduism and particularly to the matter of unity and diversity. The term 'Hinduism' implies a unified system, and some modern accounts by both Hindus and non-Hindus describe it in this way. Others, however, say there are many Hindu traditions, even many 'hinduisms': they are related to one another, but remain different in important ways. Is it possible to say who is right, and to give a watertight definition of Hinduism? Until the final chapter I will follow conventional usage and refer to 'Hinduism'.

Seeing Hinduism from Different Perspectives

Returning to the focus of this chapter, I shall begin by raising a related methodological question. A methodological question is one which asks about *how* we do something – in this case, how people study Hinduism. My question is, 'Do people who practise Hinduism see it in the same way as those who study it?' For the sake of ease, I shall refer to these two groups as *devotees* and *scholars*, although it will soon become apparent that the picture is more complex than is implied by this distinction.

Why consider the differing perspectives of devotees and scholars? There are two reasons. First, in order to choose between the various books available in the 'Religion' section of the library or bookshop, it is useful to understand how those written by scholars and devotees differ. The two groups often have different intentions and readerships in mind. The former may wish primarily to inform; the latter, to encourage spiritual progress. The second reason relates to this particular book. Despite being an introduction, it is nevertheless scholarly rather than devotional. Its aim is not to recommend Hindu practices or ideas, nor is

1. Learning about Hinduism through participation. Dr Ursula King with her family and other local children at a Hindu ritual in Leeds, 1976

it to put forward a particular Hindu viewpoint, but rather to introduce interested readers – Hindu and non-Hindu – to some of the principal characteristics of Hinduism.

Among scholarly books, there are those by *insiders* and *outsiders*, Hindus and non-Hindus. In the West, for example, introductions to Hinduism are available by those who have studied and written about their own religion, like K. M. Sen, Anantanand Rambachan, and Arvind Sharma. There are others by those who have spent many years studying Hinduism but who are not Hindus themselves, like Klaus Klostermaier and Gavin Flood. Does it matter that Sen, Rambachan, and Sharma are Hindus and Klostermaier and Flood are not? To what extent does a person's religious persuasion affect what he or she writes about religion?

In fact, each book on Hinduism differs as a result of the background and viewpoint of its author. Some Hindu writers may be ardent practitioners or devotees; others may consider religion to be of little personal importance. Equally, for some non-Hindus a religious commitment (albeit to another religion) may strongly inform their scholarship, whereas for others the attempt to leave personal religious beliefs on one side is thought to be an important starting point. Not that writers always tell their readers how they stand on this issue. In the past, many Western scholars believed it was possible to provide a wholly accurate and objective account of Hinduism, in the manner of natural scientists observing and recording data. Today, most scholars of religion, like those in some other branches of scientific enquiry, concede that personal differences do have an impact on research and writing. What scholars choose to include or exclude in their books, what examples they give, and how they organize their material are all subjective decisions.

So how might my account differ from those of other authors of introductory books on Hinduism? As this is 'a very short introduction', a great deal has been left out. For example, I have chosen to write more about contemporary forms and expressions of Hinduism than the history of the religion and its early beliefs and practices. As a woman scholar, I have tried to ensure that Hindu women and those from other poorly represented groups are given sufficient attention. As a white British person, I am historically related to the colonizers of India. I can't change my heritage, but I have tried to think critically about the impact of the British on modern Hinduism. Additionally, I am a Quaker by religion, not a Hindu: what I have written is not intentionally influenced by my own religious identity, but neither is it motivated by a Hindu viewpoint. As an outsider, I offer a different perspective. I can't draw upon an internal Hindu source of knowledge, so I depend instead upon listening to many Hindu views and opinions for my understanding of the religion in all its complexity. I hope this will come across in the account which follows.

All writers have their own viewpoint. Readers do too. Those who pick up this book, for example, will already have ideas about religion in general and perhaps about Hinduism in particular. Some of you will be Hindus, others of another faith, and some of none. Equally, those of you who are students will have a scholarly interest in Hinduism, while others will thankfully not have to write essays or think about the religion analytically, but will just want to know more about it. I hope there will be something for every type of reader, even if it is only something to argue with.

The Search for Origins

To understand more about differences between the opinions of devotees and scholars, and within these two camps, let's take the example of early Indian history. This will also have the benefit of introducing some of the ideas associated with the historical development of Hinduism. (See also the timeline at the end of the book.)

How do Hindus understand their origins and the early formation of their religion? Many describe Hinduism as *sanatana dharma*, the eternal tradition or religion. This refers to the idea that its origins lie beyond human history, and its truths have been divinely revealed (*shruti*) and passed down through the ages to the present day in the most ancient of the world's scriptures, the *Veda*. Many share this faith perspective, but various differing views arise when it comes to interpreting human history in early India. A popular view today among some Hindus – particularly those who are often referred to as Hindu nationalists, owing to their belief that Hinduism is India's true religion – is that divine truth was revealed to the Aryans, whom they see as the noble, enlightened race which lived in India thousands of years ago. The Aryans shared a great language, Sanskrit, in which the Vedic scriptures were composed, and built a majestic Hindu civilization, the rituals, literature, and law of which remain the common culture of Hindus today and India's rightful national heritage. According to this view, people belonging to the religions which developed in India after the time of the Aryans, like Buddhists, Jains, and Sikhs, are all embraced as part of the Hindu religion. But many Hindus, as well as Buddhists, Jains, and Sikhs themselves, do not share this understanding. They challenge the idea that the roots of Hinduism were entirely Aryan. They believe instead that some of the great deities and important religious developments that we now associate with Hinduism came from indigenous people who lived in India before the Aryans. According to them, the latter were incomers, migrating into north-west India, conquering peaceful, settled communities, imposing their ideology yet absorbing what was valuable and popular from the surrounding culture. This has also been a widely held view among Western scholars, who have dated the Aryan migration to about 1500 BCE and the *Rig Veda*, the earliest known scripture of the Aryans, to about 1200 BCE.

In addition to those who hold one of these two broad views, there are many other Hindus whose reconstruction of early Indian history derives from the particular teachings of the Hindu group or sect to which they belong. In short, there is no single devotional perspective. Equally, scholars have differing views. The material evidence, from archaeological remains and early texts, does not provide a clear picture, and many questions remain unanswered for devotees and scholars alike.

Earlier this century, for example, British and Indian archaeologists uncovered the remains of several early cities in what was then north India (now Pakistan) which they dated to 2500–1800 BCE, a period before the time when Aryan migrants were thought to have entered north-west India. The society and culture attributed to these cities is now referred to as the Indus valley civilization (denoting its location) or the Harappan civilization (Harappa being one of the two major cities, Mohenjo-daro being the other). The religion of these cities involved temple rites, fertility rituals, the use of animals, perhaps for sacrifice, and ritual bathing in a large pool constructed of stone. Tiles or seals have been found depicting an as yet undeciphered script and religious symbols of various kinds.

Is the seated, horned figure surrounded by animals found on one seal an early depiction of the god Shiva? Are the many female figurines found in the cities and neighbouring villages merely fertility symbols, or are they evidence of a form of goddess worship which has continued unabated throughout the centuries and is still found today? Is the Indus script an early relative of Sanskrit and thus an Indo-European language, or is it a Dravidian language spoken and written by early indigenous people? Was the urban civilization of the Indus valley surpassed by the pastoral society and culture of Aryan migrants, or were all or some of the inhabitants of the cities of Harappa and Mohenjo-daro themselves Aryan?

Indian and Western indologists are actively researching these and other questions in the hope of shedding more light on the early history of India. Another group of Indian scholars uses astronomical data and calculations to date events mentioned in early texts. But how interested people – whether scholars or devotees – then interpret their new information and ideas is not a simple matter. They often have theories of their own into which they fit such new data. Scholars often claim that they are guided solely by the available evidence in drawing their conclusions, but we need only to look back to the early scholarly work by Westerners in India to see how the ideological interests of the time may have affected their work.

Most of the eighteenth- and early nineteenth-century scholars (we often refer to them as 'orientalists') who first undertook the translation of Sanskrit texts and the reconstruction of the Aryan past were also British administrators. In this capacity, they needed to acquire a good understanding of Hindu culture and traditions in order to help in the establishment of British colonial rule in India. Inspired by what they learnt about the similarities between Sanskrit and European languages and about the Aryan people described in the Sanskrit texts, some of them drew conclusions about the common origins of Indo-European societies and cultures. The romantic view which they put forward was appealing to some people in Europe and India because it suggested a common descent from noble (*arya*) origins. With its roots in early Western scholarship, it was this view, of a great Aryan race and civilization, that later became popular with Hindu nationalists. The leaders of a late nineteenth-century Hindu movement called the Arya Samaj were among the first to look back to such a golden age and to claim a continuous, unified history for selected Hindu beliefs, values, and practices from that time. What had originally been a colonial scholarly perspective was taken up by this and other groups whose religious and political views it matched.

There is a great desire among many Indians and those who study India to understand her past and to resolve these difficult questions. But it is not just a matter of uncovering more historical information in order to complete the jigsaw. It is often the case that new discoveries, while answering some questions, throw up other ones. A complete picture rarely emerges at all, and there is always room for further speculation and hypothesis. What is more, devotional understandings of early history follow their own rules, not those of scholarly evidence and argument. They are guided first and foremost by revelation. Where historical evidence can support a devotional view, it may be welcomed, but a firm religious conviction does not require such evidence in order to thrive. It depends rather on faith. For some Hindus, then, all this argument about what happened in early India is only relevant where it accords with what the scriptures tell them. However, as we have seen, there are plenty of modern Hindus who feel strongly that scholarly theories and historical data offer important support for what they believe.

What happened in the early history of India is just one of a number of controversial areas which highlight such differences of opinion. I will briefly mention two others: the dating and meaning of scripture, and the significance of practical Hinduism.

Understanding Scripture

As we have seen, for devout Hindus the *Veda* is revealed and as such does not originate at a particular time in history but is eternal and of divine origin. Hindu philosophers such as Shankara and Ramanuja, whose ideas we will look at in Chapter 3, accepted this belief and took it as a cornerstone for their ideas about the relationship between the divine and human. Western textual scholars, however, have been guided by quite different impulses. Those who have studied the *Bhagavad-gita*, the best known of all Hindu scriptures, have been motivated by the principle of scientific rigour in their attempt to date the text, to translate it accurately, and, as they see it, to let it speak for itself rather than reflect the concerns of later interpreters. Some have then gone on to challenge the accuracy of devotional translations and interpretations. Recently, however, Hindu critics have questioned their approach and its failure to give significance either to the role of revelation in Hindu belief or to the tradition of devotional commentary. Some of these critics think the Western scholarly approach of critical reasoning itself distorts the meaning of scripture. They say that revealed texts are only fully understood by those who accept their place within a dynamic, living tradition where verses and stories are heard, repeated, remembered, and passed down. In the next chapter, Hindu scriptures and their significance will be discussed in more detail.

Debating Hindu Practices

Those orientalists who first studied the religion of the Hindus in the eighteenth and nineteenth centuries were strongly influenced by preconceived notions about religion. Their own experience was of Christianity, a religion characterized by belief in God and his son Jesus, and in God's word revealed in the Bible. They expected the Hindu religion to be similar. So, it is perhaps not surprising that they focused upon religious texts such as the *Rig Veda* and *Bhagavad-gita* and the teachings and laws they contained. They were less interested in the rituals and worldly activities of the Hindus. Where they mentioned them, they often interpreted them critically as later additions to what was originally a noble belief system. These scholars intellectualized Hinduism, often describing Hindu practices as superstitious and idolatrous, and believing that Hinduism would be a better religion if they were to be removed and the theistic, philosophical, and spiritual elements stressed. Some nineteenth-century Hindu leaders were themselves influenced by such views. Ram Mohan Roy, sometimes referred to as the father of modern Hinduism, was opposed to 'idol-worship', 'polytheism', and 'widow-burning' (*sati*). He wrote in favour of monotheism, belief in one God rather than many, using selected Hindu scriptures and Christian Unitarianism to support his case. He founded a society, the Brahmo Samaj, which was committed to the reform of Hindu practices and the propagation of ideas which bridged Christian and Hindu thought. A few Western-educated Hindus accepted these ideas, but the majority did not. Orthodox brahmins defended their traditions. They were joined by a Western scholar, H. H. Wilson, who argued that rituals like *sati* were part of Hindu tradition and should not be meddled with by interfering, though well-meaning, outsiders.†

One writer, Nirad Chaudhuri, who has written with energy about these debates, concludes that Hinduism is not defined so much by its spiritual and philosophical traditions as by its *worldliness*, its focus on the things of this world like the acquisition of wealth and love and the practice of duty. He argues that the ritual, devotional, and social practices of the followers of Krishna, Shiva, and the Goddess have too often been ignored in Western accounts. An important aspect of Hinduism, he

† See Chapter 6 for further discussion of Ram Mohan Roy, Western orientalists, and the debate about *sati*.

believes, is power. Its adherents are concerned with seeking divine assistance in order to acquire and use this power for desired ends and rewards.

We have seen that scholars and devotees have often been motivated by different principles in their ideas about Hinduism, its history, scriptures, and practices. But there have also been differences within each camp. Some non-Hindu scholars have tried imaginatively to enter Hindu world-views, whereas others have viewed them through the lens of their own colonial or Christian interests. Some Hindus have developed a sense of critical distance towards their religion which enables them to consider it more objectively, while others have been nurtured by traditional Hindu means and see no reason to question what they have been taught. In the next chapter, we shall look more closely at the way Hindus learn about their traditions and the value they place upon retaining them and passing them on to the next generation.

Chapter 2

Revelation and the Transmission of Knowledge

Storytellers and *Shankara-acharyas*: Handing down Hindu Teachings

Sitting bolt upright, cross-legged on the cool clay-washed floor of his house, he may be seen any afternoon poring over a ponderous volume in the Sanskrit language mounted on a wooden reading stand, or tilting towards the sunlight at the doorway some old palm-leaf manuscript. When people want a story, at the end of their day's labours in the fields, they silently assemble in front of his home, especially on evenings when the moon shines through the coconut palms . . . he is completely self-reliant, knowing as he does by heart all the 24,000 stanzas of the *Ramayana*, the 100,000 stanzas of the *Mahabharata*, and the 18,000 stanzas of the *Bhagavata*. If he keeps a copy of the Sanskrit text open before him, it is more to demonstrate to his public that his narration is backed with authority.

The Pandit (as he is called) is a very ancient man, continuing in his habits and deportment the traditions of a thousand years . . . He has unquestioned faith in the validity of the *Vedas*, which he commenced learning when he was seven years old. It took him twelve years to master the intonation of the *Vedas* . . . Even the legends and myths, as contained in the puranas, of which there are eighteen major ones, are mere illustrations of the moral and spiritual truths enunciated in the *Vedas*. 'No one can understand the significance of any story in our mythology unless he is deeply versed in the *Vedas*,' the storyteller often declares. Everything is interrelated.

R. K. Narayan's storyteller in *Gods, Demons and Others* embodies an important Hindu notion – that traditional stories and the truths they contain are worthy of continual retelling. He is a medium or channel, one who by his public recitation brings Hindu teachings to a ready audience. His duty is great and his task important: to recite the age-old stories from the scriptures, to thrill his audience with tales of Rama and Sita, Radha and Krishna, to show their contemporary relevance, and to continue the chain of storytelling from his father and grandfather. His work embodies the notion of tradition and its continuity from generation to generation. Like some other Hindu specialists, he imparts what he himself once learnt.

The Sanskrit word for this is *sampradana*, meaning 'giving' or 'teaching'. A related term is *sampradaya*, oral tradition, which is generally used to indicate an institution centred around a guru in which theological and ritual traditions are passed down and sustained from generation to generation. There are many *sampradayas* in contemporary Hinduism, some of which we will learn more about in the next chapter, and which are linked to early teachers by means of a lineage or chain of disciples. One example is the *sampradaya* formed by a ninth-century teacher, Shankara, which continues today in several monastic institutions in different parts of India. These are places of great learning where monks train in Sanskrit and philosophy, and where ordinary Hindus come to worship and to seek guidance from a guru. They are headed by renowned leaders known as *Shankara-acharyas* (*acharya* means 'leader' or 'master'). Before taking on the mantle of religious authority, these leaders receive a traditional training undertaken by many brahmin boys in which they learn to recite Vedic texts. As youths they are also instructed by their gurus in the teachings of the *sampradaya*. Once selected as future leaders, they travel for many years as gurus in their own right, giving spiritual advice and helping people to carry out their religious duties. They are then initiated into the role and responsibilities of *Shankara-acharya*. They are known for their personal charisma, wisdom, and piety, but they are also the bearers of the great tradition of Shankara, assisting the passage of his teachings through the generations.

The *Shankara-acharyas* are brahmins; they are also gurus. In both capacities they fulfil the important function of handing down knowledge. Although the two roles are brought together in the *Shankara-acharya* and in some other important teachers, this is not always the case. Gurus may come from any caste group, and brahmins need not be spiritual guides, though many are. What brahmins and gurus transmit and how they do so may be quite different, as we shall see shortly.

Shruti and *Smriti*: Revelation and Tradition

In the previous chapter I referred to the important concept of *shruti*, that which is revealed. It refers to the manifestation of the divine in the world, particularly to the truths revealed to the early sages or *rishis* which were later brought together in the form of scriptures. There are different views among Hindus about which scriptures are *shruti* and which fall into the other important category of sacred literature, *smriti*, that which is 'remembered' or 'handed down'. *Smriti* texts are based upon revealed truth, but are of human composition. A common division between the early texts is set out on p. 16.

The *Vedas* and *Upanishads* constitute the *shruti* literature and are said to have been divinely revealed; the Epics, *Puranas*, and *Sutras* are said to have been taught by sages and remembered by their disciples (*smriti*). The *Veda* contains accounts of creation, information about ritual sacrifice, and prayers to the gods. The *Rig Veda*, the earliest of the Vedic texts, is a collection of hymns to the gods. Agni, the deity associated with fire and sacrifice, was one of the most popular. As fire, Agni was prayed to as one who was accessible to people and one who could bring light. He was also addressed as a messenger, the one who communicated between humanity and the other gods. Here is a hymn of invocation to him:

> I pray to Agni, the household priest who is the god of the sacrifice, the one who chants and invokes and brings most treasure. Agni earned the prayers of the ancient sages, and of those of the present too; he will bring the gods here. Through Agni one may win wealth, and growth from day to day, glorious and most abounding in heroic sons. Agni, the sacrificial ritual that you encompass on all sides – only that one goes to the gods. Agni, the priest with the sharp sight of a poet, the true and most brilliant, the god will come with the gods. Whatever good you wish to do for the one who worships you, Agni, through you, O Angiras, that comes true. To you Agni, who shine upon darkness, we come day after day, bringing our thoughts and homage to you, the king over sacrifices, the shining guardian of the Order, growing in your own house. Be easy for us to reach, like a father to his son. Abide with us, Agni, for our happiness.

Most Hindus accept the status and authority of the *Veda*, but very few have read it, although they will all have heard parts of it chanted in Sanskrit during important ceremonies. The more popular texts, which are often known intimately by Hindus, are the *Mahabharata* and the *Ramayana* (see Chapter 4). The former includes the 'Song of the Lord' or *Bhagavad-gita*, in which Krishna teaches the warrior Arjuna about the importance of doing one's duty and about how to achieve liberation from suffering and repeated rebirth. So beloved are the Epics that they are sometimes referred to as a fifth *Veda* and considered to be divinely revealed.

Other types of literature are important, too, and are given varying status by different groups of Hindus. The *Tantras*, texts from the eighth and ninth centuries which focus on spiritual discipline, ritual activity,

Hinduism

Shruti	Smriti

Veda: There are four collections which comprise the *Veda*. They are known as *Rig Veda*, *Sama Veda*, *Yajur Veda*, and *Atharva Veda*. The first three contain hymns and mantras; the fourth, spells and charms. These are the earliest known Hindu scriptures.

There are three other types of *shruti* literature: the *Brahmanas*, the *Aranyakas* and, of most importance, the *Upanishads*.

Upanishads: The word *upanishad* means 'sitting near' and implies that these texts were secret scriptures taught by a sage to a disciple. The principal *Upanishads* include *Brihadaranyaka*, *Chandogya*, *Katha*, *Maitri*, and *Shvetashvatara*.

Shruti scriptures are commonly dated by scholars between 1500 and 300 BCE. They were all composed in Sanskrit.

Epics: The earliest scriptures identified as *smriti* are the *Mahabharata* – which includes the *Bhagavad-gita* – and the *Ramayana*, dated between 500 BCE and 100 CE. These are long poems which narrate episodes in the lives of great warriors. Krishna appears in the first; Rama has a central role in the second.

Sutras: In the same period, a number of texts about important subjects such as *dharma*, *yoga*, and *Vedanta* were composed (see the glossary). They contained statements or aphorisms (*sutra* means 'thread'). An important text from this period was the *Manusmriti*, which dealt with Hindu law and conduct.

Puranas: Mythological texts known as *Puranas* followed in the period from 300 to 900 CE. They refer to earlier events, often telling the stories of the gods and goddesses. Principal texts include *Markandeya Purana*, *Vishnu Purana*, *Vayu Purana*, *Shiva Purana*, and *Bhagavata Purana*.

and the attainment of magical powers, and often take the form of a dialogue between Shiva and the Goddess, are acclaimed in Kashmir, Bengal, and Nepal. They are significant for heterodox Tantric Hinduism, which has special doctrines and rituals that differ from those of the brahmins. Translated into Tamil, these texts (sometimes known as *Agamas*) now also have a ceremonial use among south Indian brahmins who consider them to complement Vedic texts. Devotional or *bhakti* poetry, composed in local Indian languages, is also popular. One notable example is the collection of Tamil songs to the god Vishnu by the tenth-century poet Nammalvar from south India. Such is its stature, it is often referred to as the 'Tamil *Veda*'.

According to R. K. Narayan's storyteller, all India's myths and stories derive their significance and authority from the *Veda*. Many Hindus would agree with him, seeing later Tantric and devotional texts as a culmination of the *Veda*; others would see them rather as a challenge to Vedic religion. However, so great is the importance of the *Veda* in the authorization of many later scriptures and in brahminical orthodoxy that some commentators have seen it as the defining aspect of Hinduism. In an important text on Hindu law from the second century BCE, called the *Manusmriti*, the author, Manu, declared that the *Veda* should not be questioned and that those who did so were beyond the pale. A modern American scholar, Brian K. Smith, has suggested that Hindus are those people who use the *Veda* as a reference point for the creation, maintenance, and transformation of their traditions. By this definition, Buddhists, Jains, and Sikhs, who deny Vedic authority and the role of brahmins in conveying and interpreting it, are clearly not within the Hindu fold.

The Brahmin and the Transmission of Ritual Knowledge

Although the concepts of *shruti* and *smriti* refer to sacred literature, they are also important for understanding the figures mentioned earlier in

Brahman, *Brahmin*, Brahmanas, Brahma

With so many similar words, it is easy for confusion to arise about their application and meaning. Here is a guide:

brahman: This originally referred to creative power or truth, inherent in Vedic hymns and later in the sacrifice during which they were recited. By the time of the early *Upanishads*, it had come to refer to the impersonal cosmic principle or absolute reality.

brahmin: A ritual specialist associated with *brahman*; one who recites Vedic hymns and performs the sacrifice; priestly caste. Also known as *brahmana* and *brahman*.

Brahmanas: Texts having to do with *brahman* in which Vedic sacrifice is described.

Brahma: The Hindu god associated with creation.

this chapter and their religious roles. Brahmins, gurus, and storytellers, in their different ways, are all channels for the truth once revealed, then remembered and orally transmitted through history. The hymns of the *Veda*, which were heard and recited by the early sages, became the responsibility of brahmin families who passed them on from father to son, unchanged down the centuries (to recipients like Narayan's storyteller). In a famous verse from *Rig Veda* 10.90 the class of people known as brahmins were identified with the mouth of the cosmic person, Purusha; his arms, thighs, and feet becoming the other classes of society (*varna*). The brahmins were thus linked in Vedic society with language and communication, with the recitation of Vedic hymns and formulas (*mantra*), and, ultimately, with the sacred power inherent within them.

Varna, social class	*Ashrama*, stages of life
The four traditional Aryan social classes (*varna*) were identified in *Rig Veda* 10.90 with parts of the body of the cosmic Purusha:	Four stages of life were described in later Hindu texts, though originally they were seen not as stages but as alternative life-choices. Only 'twice-born' males undertook the four *ashramas*, which were the stages of:
mouth – brahmins (*brahmana*)	
arms – warriors (*kshatriya*)	
thighs – commoners (*vaishya*)	student (*brahmacharya*)
feet – servants (*shudra*)	householder (*grihastha*)
The *varnas* were organized hierarchically. The first three classes were called 'twice-born', with boys being given a sacred thread in an initiation ceremony (*upanayana*). Only 'twice-born' males were entitled to hear the *Veda*. The *shudra* class was probably added to the others in order to accommodate the local non-Aryan population.	forest dweller (*vanaprastha*)
	renouncer (*sannyasa*)
	Following their early years in their father's home, young women were married. Marriage was seen as their rite of initiation into the duties of a wife.

When British administrators first conversed with brahmins in India in the eighteenth century they were astonished to find that Vedic scriptures had been passed down accurately in oral form – not learnt from written texts – by the ancient process of transmission, where brahmin boys in the student stage of life learnt by imitation of their elders. Even today, some young brahmins learn to recite Vedic mantras

2. Brahmin conducting a ritual at a pilgrimage site

in the traditional way, though modern printing and secular education have led to the scriptures being read by many people in new ways.

However, these brahmin males do not only recite Vedic mantras for their own sake, to keep divine revelation alive; they also carry out rites to sustain the world and to maintain the relationship between humanity and the gods. They are associated with *dharma*, which is sometimes

Varna-ashrama-dharma

Although *dharma* has several important meanings, in this context it means the duties or obligations which fall to a person according to his particular social class and stage of life. Men who were not 'twice-born' and had no access to Vedic teaching were not expected to follow the same stages of life as those in the higher classes. Married women's obligations were generally referred to as *stri-dharma*, the duties of the wife.

translated as religion, but more properly as truth, law, duty, or obligation. *Dharma* has a general and a personal application. The harmony of the world must be maintained, and an individual's *dharma* must be fulfilled. The work of the brahmin supports both of these requirements. By performing sacrificial rituals (*yajna*) similar to those mentioned in the *Veda*, brahmins make offerings to the gods in the sacred fire and petition them to sustain the natural world and benefit their patrons. Then, in special rites associated with the life cycle (*samskara*), they initiate Hindus into new roles. By giving the sacred thread in the *upanayana* ceremony, they convey the status of 'twice-born' upon young males. In marriage they bind together husband and wife and set them off on the householder stage of life. In rites surrounding childbirth they ensure the correct entry into society of the new-born baby and help to rid the family of the pollution arising from the birth. And, finally, in the ceremonies associated with death, they facilitate the smooth transition of the soul and make sure the ancestors are correctly served.

Brahmins are not involved in the disposal of the body of the deceased as this is considered too polluting a task for one whose power derives in part from his ritual purity. Similarly, there are other rituals outside their sphere of activity, such as the propitiation or exorcism of dangerous spirits. Ritual specialists from other caste groups for whom purity is not so important are responsible for these. They, too, may have inherited the necessary practical knowledge and mantras from their caste elders.

The Guru and the Transmission of Spiritual Knowledge

The author R. K. Narayan was very interested in religious figures, their social position, charisma, and authority. In *The Guide* he wrote about an ex-prisoner who, taking shelter in a temple one day after his release from jail, is mistakenly thought to be a holy man. He finds himself giving advice and telling homiletic stories (remembered from his mother's

The Indian Caste System (*Jati*)

Strictly speaking, class (*varna*) and caste (*jati*) are different social institutions, though castes are often assumed to fit into the four *varnas*. *Jati*, which means 'birth', is a system of social divisions organized according to relative purity, with brahmins at one extreme and low caste and 'untouchable' people (who are considered impure and polluting to 'higher' castes) at the other. Although the caste system is not one based on wealth, with those at the top being the richest, it is certainly the case that those at the bottom (the untouchables) have little access to resources. They rarely own land and have little economic power.

Indians acquire caste status by being born into a particular caste group; they generally marry someone from the same caste. In earlier times, castes were also occupational groups, though urbanization and industrialization have meant that many people are now working in quite different jobs to those with which they were traditionally associated. Because of the link between purity, pollution, and caste, a person's caste can also influence their social relationships, particularly with whom they may eat and where they live. Untouchables are often forced to live outside the village, away from those of higher castes. The Constitution of India outlawed untouchability and it was made a punishable offence in the 1950s, but change has been very slow and the situation of India's untouchables continues to be a social ill in need of urgent treatment (see also Chapter 7).

knee), then fasting to bring an end to the drought which endangers the livelihood of the villagers. He is held in awe, assumed to be above temptation and weakness, to be able to intercede with God, and to have spiritual gifts arising from his ascetic practices. He is thought to be wise and to know what is best for people. These are some of the characteristics often associated with a guru, one who can enlighten others and can help them cross the ocean of repeated death and rebirth (*samsara*) to gain liberation (*moksha*).

Who is fitted for this task? Does it require the Sanskrit training of the brahmin or the storyteller's knowledge of mythology? As Narayan's guide shows, the key to a guru's authority lies in charisma rather than in caste tradition, formal training, or even virtue. Some gurus have no secular or Vedic education. Some are illiterate. But they all have the knowledge acquired through their own spiritual experience plus a profound ability to use this to good effect in helping others.

Anandamayi Ma was one such guru. She was born in a village in what is now Bangladesh in 1896 and, despite marrying and becoming a housewife, she became a spiritual practitioner and guide to many. She was different in many ways to the *Shankara-acharyas* described earlier because she was not part of a traditional institution. She was not formally initiated, nor was she trained in her youth for religious responsibilities. While she was from a brahmin household, as a woman, she had not been given a Vedic education, but had been married when she was 13 years old.

For several years after settling with her husband's family she regularly chanted the names of God and sat in meditation, often becoming fully absorbed and unaware of what went on around her. Then, when she was 26, she had an extraordinary experience of inner initiation (*diksha*) in which she believed she was given her own mantra, a word or verse on which she could meditate. In a deep sense, as she reported later, she

3. Guru and disciples: Nilima Devi conveys the spirit of the dance to her pupils

came to realize that the guru, the disciple, and the mantra were all one. They were not separate.

This realization bears a strong resemblance to that described by some other Hindu mystics. It is also that which is identified by philosophers in the tradition of Shankara as an experience of *brahman*, the one absolute reality that is at once the universal principle and the self or spiritual aspect of each person (see Chapter 3). However, Anandamayi Ma was not concerned with philosophical speculation or debate, but rather with witnessing to the truth and helping those who sought her out. Like so many other gurus, she travelled extensively, meeting disciples of all castes and sharing her observations. She spoke practically, alluding to the natural world, relationships, and ordinary life. Her advice to people on how to make spiritual progress was simple and undemanding: she invited them to find a regular time to commit themselves to the truth, a time when they would endeavour to be moderate in their habits, would serve others as manifestations of the divine, and would strive for tranquillity. She encouraged them to do as she had done, to chant or meditate, and gradually to realize their own true nature.

She passed on the knowledge she had acquired through her own experience in much the same way as Hindu mothers do when they tenderly nurture their children in the rituals and stories handed down within their own families. She was referred to by many, including those of other religions, as 'Ma' or mother. But, like other gurus, she was also childlike, revelling in her experience of the divine and joyfully sharing it with others.

Anandamayi Ma represents the continuity of a tradition from the time of the *Upanishads* or earlier in which a disciple seeks wholeheartedly for spiritual truth and is guided by the inner self to enlightenment. She is said to have attained what is known as *jivanmukti*, liberation within this life. She became one who was sought out by others for the wisdom she could impart. In the next chapter we shall learn more about how this inner self and the truth it reveals are understood in Hinduism.

Chapter 3
Understanding the Self

Twentieth-century gurus have continued to teach and guide their disciples by traditional methods while also employing up-to-date techniques of communication, principally the printed word, modern means of transport, and, more recently, computers and the Internet. A number of gurus maintain an international following in this way. Successful guru-based groups such as the Swaminarayan Hindu Mission, the International Society for Krishna Consciousness (ISKCON), and the Shaiva Siddhanta Movement have centres in and beyond India, with their leaders travelling around the globe to visit disciples. The last of these is a south Indian movement led in the West by a guru called Sivaya Subramuniyaswami, who is American by birth and *Shaiva* Hindu by initiation. He has used the medium of a globally distributed newspaper, *Hinduism Today*, to reach established and potential disciples and other interested people. Anyone who wants to know his thoughts on the nature and destination of the self may find them by searching the archive of *Hinduism Today* on the Internet. From the 'Publisher's Desk' in the November 1996 issue, Sivaya Subramuniyaswami gives his answer to the question 'Who Am I?':

> Rishis proclaim that we are not our body, mind or emotions. We are divine souls on a wondrous journey. We came from God, live in God and are evolving into oneness with God. We are, in truth, the Truth we seek. Aum.

We are immortal souls living and growing in the great school of earthly experience in which we have lived many lives. Vedic rishis have given us courage by uttering the simple truth, 'God is the Life of our life.' A great sage carried it further by saying, there is one thing God cannot do: God cannot separate Himself from us. This is because God is our life. God is the life in the birds. God is the life in the fish. God is the life in the animals.

Becoming aware of this Life energy in all that lives is becoming aware of God's loving presence within us. We are the undying consciousness and energy flowing through all things.

Those disciples who have committed themselves to following the teachings of this guru may also approach him directly by e-mail, asking their own questions about the soul or self. Here, we have a new version of the old idea found in the *Upanishads*, of a seeker enquiring of a sage about the truth. A deeper relationship must await the initiation of the disciple by the guru, but initial answers to existential and practical questions can be obtained by a seeker irrespective of distance and regardless of caste, nationality, gender, or religion.

To explore further Hindu ideas about the self, it is helpful to go back to a much earlier story in which a disciple is instructed by his guru. Picture a disciple, a young man in his twenties called Shvetaketu, and his teacher, who is none other than his father, Uddalaka Aruni. Shvetaketu has already studied the *Vedas* and, thinking himself learned, has returned to his father's home. There, his father discovers that, despite years of study, his son has not fully comprehended the true nature of reality. Using the analogy of the fig, Uddalaka demonstrates how the same essence is in everything: the quality of the fig is in the fruit, the seeds within it, and the tree which grows from it. To press his point further, the father then instructs his son using the example of salt:

'Put this chunk of salt in a container of water and come back tomorrow.'

The son did as he was told, and his father said to him: 'The chunk of salt you put in the water last evening – bring it here.' He groped for it but could not find it, as it had dissolved completely.

'Now, take a sip from this corner,' said the father. 'How does it taste?'

'Salty.'

'Take a sip from the centre. – How does it taste?'

'Salty.'

'Take a sip from that corner. – How does it taste?'

'Salty.'

'Throw it out, and come back later.' He did as he was told and found that the salt was always there. The father told him: 'You, of course, did not see it there, son; yet it was always right there. The finest essence here – that constitutes the self of this whole world; that is the truth; that is the self (*atman*). And that's how you are, Shvetaketu!'

Upanishads: Chandogya Upanishad, 6.13.

'That's how you are' is a translation of a famous Sanskrit phrase, 'Tat tvam asi'. It expresses the idea that the truth which underlies everything and is its essence is also identical with Shvetaketu's own self (*atman*). This truth or self is the life force (*brahman*) within both the world and humanity. These three important words, 'Tat tvam asi', are considered to contain a vital truth about the nature of reality, and to have the power to bring about self-realization. As well as appearing in the *Upanishads*, this and other important phrases are found in a later compendium of aphorisms known as the *Brahma-sutra* or *Vedanta-sutra*. This text summarized the teachings of the *Upanishads* on ultimate reality (*brahman*), and became pivotal within a philosophical system known as *vedanta* (see p. 30). *Vedanta* was one of six orthodox systems (*darshana*) within Hinduism; the *yoga* system was another (see appendix).

To understand more about *vedanta*, and particularly what it teaches about the self, we will look briefly at how three philosopher-theologians understood the self, and at how their ideas have continued to be significant for modern Hindu movements. Shankara, Ramanuja, and Madhva were south Indian brahmins who were acknowledged for their skill in philosophical exposition. They became known for their differing approaches to *vedanta*. Each offered a different interpretation which, while consistent with *vedanta* tradition, was pertinent to the time in which he lived. We will learn more about them shortly, but first we shall consider their relevance for contemporary Hinduism.

When Westerners were first introduced to Hindu spirituality at the end of the nineteenth century by a travelling teacher called Vivekananda (see also Chapter 6), what they encountered was a modern interpretation of Shankara's ideas about *vedanta*. From him they learnt that the impersonal, ultimate reality was also the personal God that people worshipped, and that this God was also the higher self within each human being: 'He is you yourself,' said Vivekananda (echoing 'Tat tvam asi').

This modern version of Shankara's non-dualist *vedanta* became so widespread in the West that many commentators assumed it to be synonymous with Hinduism as a whole. They weren't aware that there were other equally persuasive and quite different perspectives on the divine and its relationship to the human self. When seekers and scholars began to visit India in large numbers in the 1960s and 1970s, they met with gurus and movements representing other approaches to *vedanta*. The widespread popularity of devotional, theistic Hinduism, underpinned by the theological ideas of Ramanuja and Madhva and their later disciples, was apparent throughout India and further afield

Vedanta and Vedantins

Vedanta is a philosophical system in which scholars have focused upon the study of Vedic texts concerning ultimate reality (*brahman*). Of particular importance for study were the *Upanishads*, the *Bhagavad-gita*, and the *Brahma-sutra*. There have been many vedantin scholars, three of whom have been especially influential in the history of Hindu thought and practice. Their views have ranged from an understanding of the relationship between ultimate reality and the self as identical (Shankara) to an understanding of their separation and difference (Madhva).

Shankara (788–820 CE) Non-dualist or *advaita vedanta*	Ramanuja (1017–1137 CE) Qualified non-dualist or *vishishtadvaita vedanta*	Madhva (thirteenth century CE) Dualist or *dvaita vedanta*
The Order founded by Shankara continues today in Sringeri, Dwarka, Badrinath, Puri, and Kanchi. The impact of Shankara's ideas has also been felt through Vivekananda, the Ramakrishna Order, and the Vedanta Society in the USA. Hindu mystics and scholars continue to expound *advaita vedanta*.	The Shri-Vaishnava Order of which Ramanuja was a leader, and in which his philosophy is taught, continues today with its centre in Srirangam in south India. The Gujarati Swaminarayan Movement is one of several *sampradayas* which claim disciplic succession from Ramanuja.	The temple and monastery at Udipi which were established by Madhva in the thirteenth century continue today. The International Society for Krishna Consciousness (and the Bengali Gaudiya Vaishnava Math in which it has its origins) claims a disciplic link to Madhva via the sixteenth-century charismatic figure Chaitanya.

among migrant Hindus. From the traditional Shri-Vaishnava *sampradaya* in south India to the modern movements of the Swaminarayans in Gujarat and the Hare Krishnas (ISKCON) in Bengal and beyond, the devotional theology which had challenged early non-dualist ideas about ultimate reality and the self was flourishing.

But what were these ideas, and why have they been so important for the development of Hinduism?

Shankara

Advaita means 'non-duality'. Used to describe Shankara's perspective on *vedanta*, it indicates the inseparability of the salt and the water in the story about Shvetaketu. To Shankara, ultimate reality and the self were identical, and his task was to explain why people failed to realize this. One of the ways in which he did this was by referring to the example of the traveller who mistook a rope for a snake, superimposing a false impression (a snake) upon the truth (the rope). He listed the many ways in which different people understood – or rather misunderstood – the self, for example, by equating it with the body, the sense organs, or the mind. All these imposed a false idea upon the self (*atman*). To Shankara, *atman* was really none other than *brahman*. There was no plurality of consciousness or being. It was all one. Liberation was achieved by removing ignorance, learning to discriminate between what was eternal and what only masqueraded as such, and then acquiring knowledge of the self's identity with *brahman.*

To the brahminical community, Buddhism remained a significant threat in India, so Shankara cleverly borrowed scholarly methods used earlier in Buddhist philosophy in order to reassert brahminical ideas. By acknowledging a lower, conditioned level of knowledge in which distinctions, like those between the rope and the snake, were recognized, he was able to explain the importance given in the *Veda* to ritual activity and sacrifice to the gods. He distinguished this from the higher or absolute level in which all is one and reality is experienced as non-dual.

Ramanuja

Teaching more than two centuries later in another religious context, Ramanuja's task was different. Unlike Shankara, he did not have to combat the popularity of Buddhism, but was committed instead to promoting the religion of the *Vaishnavas*, the followers of the god Vishnu, by giving philosophical support to their devotional claims. Ramanuja worshipped Vishnu and was well versed in the Epics, *Puranas*, and the poetry of his region. His ideas built on the work of Shankara, which, by Ramanuja's time, was accepted by the brahmin community and considered orthodox. He agreed that ultimate reality was non-dual, but disagreed profoundly with Shankara on the nature of *brahman*, the individual selves, and the world. He was pointed in his criticisms, accusing Shankara's followers of error and a lack of insight, and building his own case with examples from a wide range of scriptures.

His main claim was that the strong conviction we have that we are different from one another and from God is not false, as Shankara claimed it to be. The conclusions of our senses and feelings are not illusory. They indicate a profound truth, that ultimate reality is internally qualified (*vishishta*). What is more, ultimate reality is not impersonal and without qualities, as Shankara asserted. Ramanuja saw it as *ishvara*, the Lord, the one who is desired by all those who seek to escape from suffering. As such, *brahman* is none other than the supreme person or God of the Epics and *Puranas*.

But what, then, is the relationship between the self and this supreme person? God is the inner controller of both the individual selves and the world. Ramanuja said that, just as the human body is the instrument of the self within, so the world and the selves are related to God.

Knowledge of God helps to lead us to liberation, but God's grace and the self's surrendering response are vital, too.

Madhva

Madhva had a good deal of sympathy with this view, but his reaction to Shankara's ideas was different again. Renouncing the world and joining a *Vaishnava* Order at 16, he learnt about *vedanta* and gradually developed his own critique (*dvaita*). Like Ramanuja, he utilized a full range of Vedic, Puranic, and later devotional texts, but went further, concluding that the teachings of scripture can only be understood as dualistic, as maintaining a complete distinction between the Lord and the self. *Brahman* and *atman* were not identical. What is more, he saw the selves as different from one another, and from the world. Even within the world, he understood phenomena to be distinct. Everything existed within the will of the supreme Lord while maintaining its own particularity. To be liberated from suffering and rebirth required divine grace, dependence on God, and active devotion, worshipping the Lord in the form of an icon (*murti*). Madhva placed such an icon of Krishna in his monastery in Udipi where it remains to be seen by pilgrims to this day.

Although each of these three philosopher-theologians composed commentaries on the key *vedanta* texts, they drew widely varying conclusions, for example, on the meaning of the phrase we encountered in the story of Shvetaketu: 'Tat tvam asi', 'That you are'. For Shankara, this signified non-duality; there was no difference between that ultimate reality and the self. For Ramanuja, unity was not implied. Instead, the sentence suggested that *brahman* (*tat*) and *atman* (*tvam*) were distinguished from one another though clearly related. For Madhva, the two were wholly separate, though he saw the self as being in God's image and inhabited by a divine inner witness.

Although these three were the most renowned of *vedantin* scholars, there were others, most of whom, like Ramanuja and Madhva, were *Vaishnavas*, extolling the glories of Vishnu or Krishna. Others, particularly those who revered the god Shiva, have worked outside the tradition of *vedanta*, drawing on Tantric texts in order to develop their theological ideas.

Today, these philosophical conclusions continue to be heard and discussed by disciples within the religious institutions associated with Shankara, Ramanuja, and Madhva. The *Shankara-acharyas* discussed in the last chapter continue to preach *advaita-vedanta*. The Shri-Vaishnavas of south India are the natural successors of the theology of Ramanuja. The monastery in Udipi still teaches the devotional dualism of Madhva. The Shaiva Siddhanta Movement mentioned at the beginning of this chapter perpetuates the theology developed by earlier *Shaiva* theologians. Earlier this century, many commentators saw Shankara's *advaita vedanta* as the epitome of Indian intellectual achievement, but, more recently, an awareness of the vitality of Hindu devotional movements has helped to reassert those theistic perspectives which focus on the loving relationship between devotees and their chosen deity.

These philosophical ideas are not really a matter for everyday discussion by the majority of Hindus, but they do underlie the way in which Hindus think about the divine. Whether a Hindu believes in an ultimate impersonal reality or a personal God has important consequences for his or her religious practice and spiritual journey. Acquiring more knowledge of ultimate reality and its relationship to the self is vital for the former; prayer and worship are central to the latter. One religious idea to which all Hindus make frequent reference, however, is *karma*.

Karma, *Yoga*, and the Self

No short discussion of Hindu views of the self would be complete without a consideration of two familiar notions, *karma* and *yoga*. They

4. Transmigration of the self

are household words, not only in India but also in the West, where *karma* is often associated with fatalism and reincarnation, and *yoga* – usually *hatha yoga* – practised to improve health and well-being. They were mentioned in the *Upanishads* and *Bhagavad-gita*, and were discussed by Shankara, Ramanuja, and Madhva. As ideas they were also known to the renouncers or sages of early India.

Anyone who knows the story of the Buddha will be aware that early Indian society in his time was viewed by a spiritual seeker as a place of misery and unrest. Happiness was transitory, to be replaced all too soon by ageing, disease, and death. As scholars have shown, it was also a time of social and political change, with towns growing up, and the agrarian lifestyle and its social organization being eroded. With urban development came greater opportunity for mobility and communication. New ideas travelled as well as people. Many of those who had renounced society to wander and practise the ascetic life shared the view that an individual's personality or self transmigrated at death to a new body, and that this cycle of rebirth (*samsara*) was fuelled by a chain of cause and effect linked to action (*karma*). All living things were subject to this, and, although good actions might bring about felicitous results and a better rebirth, the suffering and inevitability inherent in the process were seen by many as intolerable. Liberation from continual rebirth was sought, with renouncers attempting by various means to break the cycle, by isolating themselves from society, undergoing fasting and mortification, surrounding themselves with the reminders of suffering and death, and withdrawing into themselves in meditation. By such means, action and its results would cease and liberation would be possible.

The problems associated with action and rebirth were addressed several centuries later in the *Bhagavad-gita*. Here, we find Arjuna enquiring of his charioteer, Krishna, about whether he should go into battle against his own kin. Krishna, who, despite his disguise, is really the supreme Lord, offers him guidance like a guru, arguing the case for dutiful action, explaining the journey of the self and the paths to its liberation. He explains to the perplexed Arjuna that the embodied self or soul does not die in battle, but passes into a new body: 'It cannot be pierced, it cannot be burned, it cannot be wetted, it cannot be parched. It is invariable, everywhere, fixed, immovable, eternal.' (2.24) He reminds Arjuna of his social and religious duty (*dharma*) as a member of the warrior class, and goes on to teach him about the discipline of action. Arjuna assumes that Krishna's view, like that of the ascetics, is that action is to be renounced.

Krishna's response comes loud and clear: 'A man does not attain freedom from the results of action by abstaining from actions, and he does not approach perfection simply by renunciation.' (3.4) He goes on to explain that it is the results of action which are to be renounced, not action itself – one should not desire particular rewards, nor think proudly of oneself as the doer of great deeds. One should be satisfied in the self, offering action and its fruits as a sacrifice to the Lord. This is the discipline of *karma yoga*. Having taught this, Krishna goes on to explain other worthy paths which, pursued steadfastly, will bring a seeker to equanimity and, finally, liberation. *Jnana yoga*, the path of knowledge, and *bhakti yoga*, the way of devotion – to which we shall return in Chapter 5 – are given particular attention by Krishna, who emerges gradually in the song as the universal Lord in whom all seekers may find shelter.

In the sixth chapter of the *Bhagavad-gita*, Krishna discusses the practice of the *yogin*, though he recommends this path only to those capable of great self-control and determination. He describes how such a person should be seated, should control his senses and urges, and should focus his mind. Concentration on the self, quelling the passions, and becoming calm are the hallmarks of this path, the goal of which is bliss. What Krishna describes here is not the more physically strenuous *hatha yoga*, in which practitioners hold difficult postures; nor is it the *siddha yoga* of adepts who have acquired the powers of levitation and telepathy, and the ability to disappear or to withstand pain. It is akin to the practice referred to by Patanjali in his *Yoga-sutra* as *raja yoga*, the royal or highest *yoga*, a meditative *yoga* in which the pinnacle of achievement is *samadhi*, deep concentration leading to liberation of the self.

In the *Bhagavad-gita* Krishna puts forward two innovative ideas: first, *karma yoga*, offering ordinary seekers the possibility of giving spiritual meaning to their everyday actions; and, second, the notion that there is not one way but many ways to liberation, with seekers finding the way most suited to their temperaments and stations. Krishna did not forget those who were traditionally marginalized by brahminical religion. Women and the low born were also recognized as seekers and invited to offer themselves, their actions, and the simple gifts of water, a flower, a leaf, or fruit to Krishna.

The *Bhagavad-gita* transforms the earlier pessimistic notion – that the results of action lead to continual rebirth and transmigration of the self – into a positive discipline for personal transformation. In more recent times, *karma* and *karma yoga* have again been endorsed. Religious nationalists like Bal Gangadhar Tilak and Mahatma Gandhi recommended *karma yoga* in India's struggle for self-rule and as a path of self-realization for busy, modern Hindus. A contemporary Hindu scholar, Arvind Sharma, has also considered their importance for rethinking the issue of caste.

In *Rig Veda* 10.90 and Chapter 2 of the *Bhagavad-gita* we were introduced to the idea of the four classes of brahminical society. Arjuna, as a warrior, was expected to do his class duty, not being tempted to mimic the duties of others just because they seemed more palatable or worthy, or less contentious. This idea of social duty was discussed in greater detail in the *Manusmriti*, where the consequences of neglecting one's duty were treated very seriously. Undutiful or *a-dharmic* actions would be punished with expulsion from one's social group or with a lower rebirth in the next life.

Arvind Sharma tackles this problem head on in *Hinduism for Our Times*. He believes that the link between *karma* and the caste-based society of India needs to be understood and transformed. As he says, 'In the standard Hindu view one's birth in a particular caste is determined by one's *karma* in a previous life.' Hindus take on a caste identity at birth, being born into a family within a particular *jati*, as the argument goes, because of actions in a previous life. The self, in absolute terms, is untainted by this, but, as each self is embodied, it finds itself within a particular caste with all the associated duties and conditions.

It is easy to be fatalistic about this state of affairs, and many Hindu teachers, following Krishna's example in the *Bhagavad-gita*, have offered spiritual recipes for tackling it. Arvind Sharma's contemporary solution goes as follows. To think fatalistically about *karma* is unhelpful when, in fact, as human beings we have the power at any moment to change our own behaviour, and thus its consequences for our future. Free will rather than fatalism characterizes the operation of *karma*. What is more, if we accept that *karma* is not so much a process of cause and effect between lives as *within a single life*, this changes things. What we do at this moment has consequences for what will happen to us in a few minutes, next week or in ten years' time. One modern life of seventy or eighty years' duration is equal to what may have been three separate lives in the past when life was short and hard (with one birth into a single caste group, where three might previously have been the norm). What becomes important in this view is not caste as an index of past-life *karma*, but present *karma* and its consequences for a person's evolving self-realization and relationships with others. Refocusing *karma* in this way, according to Sharma, undermines the importance of caste and its iniquities. A society in which everyone recognizes that they have an immediate responsibility for improving tomorrow's world rather than their next life will be one in which caste status as a measure of previous actions will disappear. It is the teachings of Krishna on the importance of acting in the world while renouncing the results of one's actions, he says, which make this possible.

Chapter 4

Divine Heroes:
The Epic Tradition

What were 80 million Indians doing at 9.30 every Sunday morning in 1987?

They were sitting down in homes and tea-shops – anywhere there was a television – to watch the unfolding drama of the god Rama, his wife Sita, and his brother Lakshmana, in the television epic, the *Ramayan*. No one was bored, even though they knew the story already. In fact, when it was concluded initially, after 52 weeks, some viewers went so far as to go on strike to demand that further episodes be produced to complete the story (and another 26 were made). On another occasion, shortly before the denouement, when the villain Ravana was to be killed, fans made long journeys to the television studio to plead for his life. This was no ordinary soap opera. Described by its now famous director, Ramanand Sagar, as a divine phenomenon, it inspired widespread devotion, even a temporary sense of national unity, with Sikhs and Muslims as well as Hindus in its cast and among its viewers. It was more akin to ritual performance than film narrative, with the actors, costumes, lines, sets, and special effects chosen and designed to create a sense of a divine world rather than a human one. The actors became identified with the gods and demons they portrayed, with people touching their feet and seeking their blessings.

This popular Indian story of Rama, told, remembered, and retold over

5. Rama and Sita from the Doordarshan television adaptation of the *Ramayana*

two and a half millennia, is known to all Hindus and to a great many other people around the world. Hindu infants hear it from parents or other relatives. Schoolchildren learn about it at the time of the festival of *Divali*. Villagers hear it from storytellers or see it enacted in folk theatre (*ramlila*) and puppet shows, and now those with televisions and video players may play and replay their favourite sequences.

Although onlookers marvelled at the phenomenal success of the TV *Ramayan*, even praised it for its ability to deliver a religious subject and ethical issues to so large an audience via a commercial medium, nevertheless it was not without its detractors. Criticisms were directed at its sentimentality, sexism, lack of subtlety, and overstated morality. Some despised the mood of national submissiveness it seemed to engender. Perhaps the most telling criticism for those interested in its religious significance was that it gave authority to a particular version of the story and its associated values and ideas.

The *Ramayana* or story of Rama exists in possibly thousands of versions. The most widely known is the one attributed to Valmiki and passed down to him by the sage Narada, but there are many other written versions and innumerable oral ones. They focus on different characters, many on Rama himself, others on Sita, and some on the demon Ravana, showing him not as evil but as strong, brave, perhaps misguided, even as an anti-hero or committed rebel. There are *Ramayanas* in scores of languages, and there are traditions of their rendition and performance in the countries of south-east Asia as well as the Indian subcontinent. Do the many different versions and genres through which the story of Rama is communicated point to a more profound diversity – of Hindu traditions, communities, and practices, indeed of 'hinduisms', related loosely to one another by a narrative thread? But this question must await consideration in the final chapter.

Later in this chapter and again in Chapter 7 we will witness the vitality of Indian epic tradition by seeing how the characters of the *Ramayana* and their actions have been understood and used by different groups. But first, an introduction to the story itself. Here is a summary of the principal events of the widely known account attributed to Valmiki.

Ramayana: the Story

Dasharatha, the king of Ayodhya, by means of sacrifice, is blessed with several sons born to his three wives. Rama, the eldest and much beloved by Ayodhya's citizens, is to succeed him as king. However, Rama's step-mother, Kaikeyi, fearing for herself and her own son Bharata, exacts a promise from Dasharatha that Rama be banished to the forest and Bharata installed as ruler. Rama, obedient to his father's reluctant request, agrees to go. Sita, his devoted wife, won by Rama in a conquest of strength, and Lakshmana, his loyal younger brother, demand to be allowed to accompany him. They leave the city, followed soon after by Bharata who pleads with Rama to return. Rama will not break his vow, and Bharata returns to Ayodhya, placing Rama's sandals on the throne and ruling as regent in his absence.

Rama, Sita, and Lakshmana settle in a hermitage after wandering in the beautiful forest and meeting its ascetic inhabitants. They are discovered there by the sister of the demon Ravana, who tries to entice Rama and destroy Sita. Wounded by Lakshmana, she hurries to her powerful brother, ruler of Lanka, and tells him what has occurred. Ravana, stirred by the account of Sita's beauty, determines to capture her. With the help of another demon, who as a deer lures away the two brothers, Ravana kidnaps Sita by disguising himself as a holy man. He takes her to his city in Lanka.

Rama and Lakshmana enlist the help of the monkeys to find and free Sita. Rama first helps the monkey prince, Sugriva, whose situation mirrors his own. Sugriva then sends his monkeys in search of Sita. It is the divine monkey Hanuman who finds her on Lanka and assures her of her forthcoming release. He is captured but escapes, returning to Rama with his intelligence of Sita's whereabouts. Rama and his army of helpers cross to Lanka on a bridge of monkeys, destroy Ravana, and return valiant with Sita. Rama is reluctant to accept Sita because of the time she has spent in Ravana's household. She undergoes an ordeal by fire to persuade him of her virtue.

Rama becomes king on their return to Ayodhya, but rumours continue about Sita's chastity. Unwillingly, Rama banishes her and she takes refuge with Valmiki (by whom this account is told). She gives birth to Rama's twin sons and later leaves the world, disappearing into the earth from which she first arose. The grieving Rama then ascends to heaven with his followers.

Dharma and the *Ramayana*

With the diverse tellings of the Rama story go different interpretations, but a common theme in many is *dharma*. As we have seen, *dharma* is an important concept in Hinduism signifying order, law, duty, and truth. Men were expected to follow their own *dharma* (their *sva-dharma*) according to their social class, *varna*, and stage of life, *ashrama*, hence the term *varna-ashrama-dharma*. The maintenance of social order in the world and the relationship between humanity and the gods were the corporate responsibility of all, though each person's behaviour in the service of *dharma* was different. The principal text in which these duties (and those of women) were codified was the *Manusmriti*, but in Valmiki's *Ramayana* we witness *dharma* played out through the righteous decisions and actions of Rama, his father, wife, brothers, and loyal devotee, Hanuman. Each has his or her own path to follow in service of the right ordering of the society to which they belong.

The *Ramayana*, like that other great epic, the *Mahabharata*, is a story about the warrior community. Brahmins and ascetics play their part, but their roles are secondary to those of Ayodhya's ruling family, and the monkey and demon warriors. It is a study of kingship, but also of human roles and relationships.

Why does Dasharatha do what Kaikeyi asks of him and banish Rama when it seems to go against the future interests of Ayodhya, and why indeed does Rama agree, in the full knowledge that its citizens want him as their king? Good order is founded on truthfulness and obedience. Dasharatha, as a husband and ruler, must not break his promise, and Rama, as a son, must obediently accept the decisions of his father. He understands his banishment as his destiny and argues against Lakshmana – who is full of indignation – by stressing the binding nature of a father's words. Rama's conduct, seen against his brother's unwillingness to accept the situation, is presented as exemplary.

Sita's behaviour and her relationship with Rama provide further opportunities for the enactment of *dharma*. A wife is not expected to fulfil *varna-ashrama-dharma*; she must fulfil her duty as a daughter, then as a wife (*stri-dharma*). Sita's decision to follow Rama into the forest, despite his protestations, and her chaste commitment to him during her time in Ravana's court are the proper actions of a devoted and dutiful wife (*dharma-patni*).

Why, then, does Rama, having seen the proof of her virtue in the fire ordeal, banish her after their return to Ayodhya? To modern, Western readers used to romantic endings this might seem heartless. But within a Hindu universe the proper ordering of society rather than the desire of the individual was of first importance. Again, Rama must think and act according to his *dharma* as king. He must give this role priority over and above his personal inclination or belief in Sita's chastity. His own failure to protect his wife from Ravana and *a-dharma* or disorder had led to doubt in the minds of his subjects, and stilling their fears and the social disorder which might follow became his primary duty, despite his knowledge of her innocence. In the Valmiki *Ramayana*, Rama is the ideal – if unhappy – king to the last. Or almost to the last, for towards the end of the story Rama is referred to as an incarnation (*avatara*) of the great god Vishnu. Like Krishna in the *Mahabharata*, Rama, as God in human form, comes into the world to vanquish the forces of *a-dharma* and to exemplify righteous conduct (see Chapter 5).

Sita, Devi, and the Goddesses

First cousin: 'Why do we not stage the fight between the good King Ram and the demon King Ravan?'

Me: 'Could I play Ram?'

Second cousin: 'No, you are a girl.'

Me: 'It is only a play.'

Third cousin: 'Why do you not play Ram's wife, the good queen, Sita?'

Me: 'But Sita does not *do* anything. She is only, well, good.'

In this conversation between the young Madhur Jaffrey – now a well-known writer and television presenter – and her male cousins, we glimpse one reaction to Sita. 'Dutiful', 'loyal', 'good', and 'beautiful' would be the qualities which might first spring to mind to describe her. But even in Valmiki's story, Sita's strength and self-possession are apparent. She is dutiful, indeed, but she has to argue her case in order to do what she knows to be right. She shows self-control and she doesn't give in to Ravana's will. On being freed, she defends herself wholeheartedly against Rama's accusations. She is far from passive.

This strength of character has not gone unnoticed by Indian women, who have found much in her to applaud. Despite being commonly held up as a paragon of the submissiveness, obedience, and loyalty that many men would like to see in their wives, women have often taken other lessons from her behaviour. 'How was it from your point of view?' asks a British Hindu poet, Debjani Chatterjee, inviting Sita to tell her side of the story. In Sita's fire ordeal Chatterjee sees the all too frequent dowry deaths of contemporary Indian women, and in her banishment she sees the trials of a modern single mother.* Sita's story, she concludes, is no fairy-tale.

In some of the other *Ramayanas* Sita takes on a still different light. In the popular Hindi version by Tulsidas she is depicted with heroic strength, being able to lift the great bow of the god Shiva. In the Tamil *Iramavataram* she is shown as justifiably angry and sarcastic, driven to verbal aggression by her harsh, accusing husband. In women's folk songs she is still more vividly portrayed. The important events of her life as a woman are told – her puberty, wedding, pregnancy, and birth of her sons – as well as what happens to her in the forest, on the island of Lanka, and during her ordeal. The words of the songs suggest that the women singers understand intimately Sita's experiences and feelings, the way in which she is misunderstood by her husband, and the trials she has to suffer. She is like them.

* For further discussion of dowry and its abuse, see Chapter 7.

Sita is a great heroine rather than a goddess. When Hindu women want to pray to a goddess or fast for her blessings, it is not Sita they choose. Parvati, the clever goddess who can intercede with Shiva, or Durga, the powerful warrior, or Santoshi Ma, the bringer of peace to the home, or Kali, the terrifying mother, are called on for help. Superhuman, they are renowned for their divine powers and their capacity to grant the requests of those who worship them. In Hindu mythology they are many, but they are also seen as expressions of the one great Devi, revered by many Hindus as their saviour and guide. Her story is told in the *Devi-Mahatmya* (part of the *Markandeya Purana*). There she is named as one who is prosperous, yet fierce and passionate, a great mother, a refuge, a divine destroyer, a benevolent goddess, a protectress. These qualities are manifest in her particular forms as Lakshmi, Durga, Amba, Kali, Parvati, and many others. But she is also given titles with universal significance. She is called *Mahamaya*, great illusion, and *Shakti*, creative power. She is associated with the supreme gods, Vishnu and Shiva, but is herself seen as the queen or sovereign one. Here is her story.

Devi-Mahatmya: the Story

Assured that he cannot be killed by any man, Mahisha, the buffalo demon, defeats the world and warns the god Indra that he will soon conquer heaven. They fight and Indra withdraws, seeking the shelter of the great gods, Brahma, Shiva, and Vishnu. They are filled with anger, and from their divine bodies a beautiful woman issues forth: Devi. They provide her with weapons; other gods give her a lion to ride and wine to drink. Her terrifying laugh is heard and the gods shout, 'Victory'.

Hearing this, Mahisha sends his demons to see what is happening. They report to him of her beauty and great qualities, and he sends her a proposal of marriage. She refuses and slays his messengers, and when Mahisha himself follows, she proclaims her mission to protect *dharma*.

6. Durga killing Mahisha, the buffalo demon

In the ensuing battle he takes many forms, but she drinks wine and, from the back of her lion, kills him with her trident and discus. The gods are full of praise for Devi's achievement.

Devi breaks the brahminical image of the woman as dutiful wife. She will not marry and cannot be controlled by male demons or gods. She is warlike and aggressive, not submissive and unassertive. She appears to be an ideal woman, being beautiful and amorous, but she drinks wine and is independent. And, in another story, she manifests the still more terrifying Kali from her angry brow, Kali emerging bedecked with severed heads and arms, dripping blood from her lolling tongue. Yet the great power of Devi can be yoked not only by the gods but also by those who praise her devoutly and make offerings to her. To such worshippers (Shaktas), though without husband or child, she is the great protective mother.

The Mother, Rama, and the Hindu Nation

The images of the protective mother and the dutiful king have inspired
loyalty and devotion in India. Both have been used in the modern period
as symbols associated with the nation. *Bharata Mata* or Mother India is a
familiar concept to Indians of many religions, drawn on earlier this
century by the Indian National Congress political party, which chose the
poem *Bande Mataram*, 'Hail Mother', as the national anthem. It is still
evoked today with the cry 'Bharata Mata ki jay', 'Long live Mother India'.

Rama is also hailed by nationalists, particularly those of a Hindu
persuasion, as divine ruler of the longed-for Hindu state. It was in
Ayodhya in north India in 1992 that a mosque was destroyed by those
Hindus who believed it to be built on the site of a more ancient temple
commemorating the birthplace of Rama. The historical facts are much
disputed, but the popular religious imagination thrives not on factual
evidence but on powerful stories and the feelings they arouse. Two
stories – one of Rama, revisited each week on television, and the other
of the presence of a Muslim place of worship on consecrated Hindu
ground – captured this imagination.

Inflamed by the campaigns of pro-Hindu groups and the rhetoric of a
Hindu nationalist political party, the mosque was destroyed. Communal
violence ensued in Indian cities, and both Muslims and Hindus died.

We have met several deities in the pages of this chapter: why are there
so many gods and goddesses in Hinduism? How is the divine presence
understood, and how is it worshipped?

Chapter 5
The Divine Presence

'Miracle', 'hallucination', 'simple scientific explanation', 'divine grace', or 'politically inspired hoax' ran the headlines as onlookers sought to explain why, on 22 September 1995, images of Ganesha the world over were devouring the milk offered to them by their devout followers. The old debate between science and faith was rekindled. Hindus themselves were quietly divided over the phenomenon, but their surprise was not so much at its occurrence as at its scale. Divine manifestations and small miracles are believed to be commonplace in Indian religious life, but that Hindus and their non-Hindu friends around the globe should witness Ganesha's gracious act was extraordinary.

Idols or Icons?

How can a statue drink? There are scientific and psychological explanations, of course, but how do Hindus explain it? First, it is important to understand the difference between statues and icons (*murtis*). The stone sculptures covering the outside of Hindu temples, the bas reliefs and cave carvings found throughout India, all vibrantly depict the iconography of the gods and goddesses and the stories of their feats. They are of great artistic merit and were lovingly carved. But only exceptionally would they be considered worthy of worship. The icon *inside* the temple, however, has been created and installed by a ritual process which has prepared it to be inhabited by God. Religious

7. A believer offers a spoonful of milk to a statue of Ganesha during the 'miracle' of September 1995

texts describe the meditative approach of the sculptor, the proportions of the icon (and the temple in which it is to be placed), and the characteristics of the deity who will reside in it. Once formed, brahmins consecrate the image, establishing various deities in different parts of its body and infusing it with living breath (*prana*). From that point on, the divine is manifest within the icon and must be cared for, served like an honoured guest, and offered love. An intimate, reciprocal relationship between devotee and deity is then possible through *darshana* or seeing. Hindus visit their local temples or take trips to more distant pilgrimage sites to take *darshana*, that is, to see and be seen by Krishna, Devi, Shiva, or another deity of their choice.

In the seventeenth and eighteenth centuries European traders and travellers first witnessed Hindus taking *darshana*. They wrote critically in their letters and diaries of 'idol-worship', and their responses were reiterated by later Christian missionaries. Such worship was considered abhorrent and misguided, particularly among Protestant Christians by whom God was apprehended in the word not the image. They were also

Ganesha

Ganesha (Ganupati) is an elephant-headed deity loved by Hindus for his kindly attentiveness to the requests of his devotees and his ability to remove obstacles. The son of Shiva and Parvati, he was created one day by his mother in order to protect her while she bathed. Shiva, unaware of his son's identity, decapitated him for failing to allow him entry to Parvati's quarters. She was very upset and Shiva promised to restore Ganesha to life with the head of the first creature to pass by. That creature was an elephant.

Ganesha is depicted with a rat, his vehicle or mount. He is rotund, and is never without a dishful of sweets.

aghast at the multiplicity of 'idols', concluding that the Hindus were a polytheistic people, believing in many separate gods and goddesses. From their perspective, though fascinating, this was erroneous. Their God, though in three persons – father, son, and holy spirit – was but one God.

These commentators did not grasp the theological reasoning behind what they saw – they simply took it at face value. In order to avoid their mistakes, we shall return briefly to the ideas of the *Vaishnava* theologians discussed in Chapter 3. Ramanuja and the *vedantins* of later centuries for whom love of Vishnu or Krishna was all-important taught that the Lord manifests in five forms: (i) in the supreme transcendental form; (ii) in its emanations (*avatara*); (iii) in the heart or self of each individual; (iv) as the inner controller of the universe; and (v) as the divine presence within the consecrated icon (*murti*). The Lord is transcendent and supreme, but also immanent and accessible. Graciously, as we saw with Rama in the *Ramayana* and Krishna in the

> 'You would scarce believe me, shou'd I name the vile and infamous creatures to which they pay divine honours. 'Tis my opinion that no idolatry among the antients was ever more gross or more horrid, than that of these Indians.'
>
> Pierre Martin, early eighteenth century.

> 'In the centre of the building was the idol, a little ugly black image, about two feet high, with a few lights burning round him . . . I shivered at being in the neighbourhood of hell . . .'
>
> Revd Henry Martyn, early nineteenth century.

Bhagavad-gita, the Lord may emanate as an *avatara* to help humanity in times of need.

He is still more approachable as the consecrated temple deity. In the Radha-Raman temple in Vrindaban, in the region of Krishna's childhood where he sported with the cowherd boys and girls and wooed Radha, he allows his devotees to serve him with loving devotion (*bhakti*) and to fulfil all his needs. With Radha, he is offered many different things including water for washing and drinking, clothes, flowers, incense, food, and praise in a ritual called *puja*. They are awoken, dressed, visited by devotees, worshipped, and put to rest each day. Within *Shaiva* and *Shakta* theology and practice, in which Shiva and Devi are respectively the focus, similar ideas and activities may be observed. However, whereas the temple icons of Vishnu, Krishna, and the goddesses have the appearance of humans (in fact, humans are made in *their* image), Shiva rarely manifests as such. He inhabits the *linga*, his sign, a smooth, cylindrical stone. *Lingas*, like icons of Krishna and Durga, are fashioned and ritually installed in temples, but they also occur naturally. Where they are found in nature they may be worshipped as Shiva despite being unconsecrated.

The Many and the One

This brings us back to Ganesha, for it was not only his temple manifestations which were said to drink the milk offered them by devotees, but also the images in people's homes. Similarly, on other occasions, pictures or images of gurus and saintly people have been seen miraculously to produce holy water or ash. Divine activities do not seem to be limited only to forms which have undergone ritual consecration. Many Hindu theologians stress both the power and grace of God or the Goddess, and this is mirrored in the non-theological imagination by an understanding that the divine may appear or give a sign at any time, to encourage or reward devotees, to warn them, even to punish them. Stories from the *Puranas*, local traditions, and anecdotal accounts of the experiences of relatives and neighbours repeat and confirm this idea.

8. A wayside shrine of Shiva and Devi

Vishnu and Shiva

From the time of the later *Upanishads*, Vishnu and Shiva became popular deities, considered worthy of worship and service by their followers, who were referred to respectively as *Vaishnavas* and *Shaivas*. Cultic practices and doctrinal teachings evolved, and in their stories or myths, recorded in the *Puranas*, they were described iconographically. Shiva was depicted as a Himalayan ascetic, Vishnu as a blue youth holding in his four hands a discus, mace, conch, and lotus. To their followers each was understood to be the supreme, transcendent Lord, but also immanent, dwelling within each person. Shiva was associated with a divine family, through whom his powers were extended. Vishnu asserted his divine influence by taking animal or human form in periods of darkness and moral degradation. By the end of the Puranic period ten principal incarnations or *avataras* had been recorded. These were:

Matsya, the fish

Kurma, the tortoise

Varaha, the boar

Narashimha, the man-lion

Vamana, the dwarf

Parashurama, Rama with the axe

Rama

Krishna

Buddha

Kalki, 'the white horse' who will come at the end of the dark age or *kali yuga*

Rama and Krishna have also been seen as independent deities, supreme in their own right. Rama is depicted as a warrior with bow and arrows, escorted by his wife Sita, brother Lakshmana, and devoted servant Hanuman, the monkey warrior. Krishna is most commonly shown as a young flute-playing cowherd boy, surrounded by cows, playing with friends, or teasing the cowherd girls (*gopis*). His favourite is Radha, and in paintings and temple iconography they are often shown together. Krishna is occasionally depicted as a mischievous baby or as the charioteer who accompanies Arjuna, hero of the *Bhagavad-gita*.

A compelling example of this is the way in which female spirits are to be found outside Indian villages, in fields, trees, rocks, and bushes. Signs of the response to their presence are witnessed everywhere: pieces of cloth tied to branches, food and other offerings left by the wayside, stones decorated with silver foil, red paint, or powder. Such signs are evidence of the propitiation of a female *bhut* or ghost, or a *mata* or local goddess. *Bhuts* are avoided for fear of their displeasure, but *matas* are worshipped to gain favours or blessings. These female spirits linger near the places where, in life, they met untimely and inauspicious deaths or died childless. Some of those women worshipped as *matas* may have ended their lives as *sati* on the funeral pyres of their husbands.

People as well as objects may reveal the presence of the supernatural. We have already seen that the self or *atman* is eternal and divine, whether it is considered to be identical with or separate from ultimate reality or God. Those whose actions show them to be self-realized are often described as *mahatmas* or great selves. Gandhi, of whom we shall hear more in the next chapter, was one of these. There are others, however, who exhibit the divine in a rather different way – through possession. Once possessed, it is not they who speak or act, but the god or goddess through them. In Kerala, at festival time, the *teyyam* deities possess brilliantly adorned dancers who then go among the assembled crowds giving *darshana*. And during *Durga Puja* in Bengal and other parts of north India, some devotees are regularly inhabited by the Goddess, who, embodied within them, may dance among her followers, answer their questions, and give them advice. Her presence in such a gathering is considered auspicious, a blessing to all.

If the divine manifests in so many forms and places, were European visitors correct in assuming that Hinduism was polytheistic? There are certainly a multitude of deities worshipped by Hindus, but if we return for a moment to the *Upanishads* we see that the many and the One are not unrelated. A seeker asks the sage Yajnavalkya how many gods there are:

'Three and three hundred, and three and three thousand.'

'Yes, of course,' he said, 'but really, Yajnavalkya, how many gods are there?'

'Thirty-three.'

'Yes, of course,' he said, 'but really, Yajnavalkya, how many gods are there?'

'Six.'

'Yes, of course,' he said, 'but really, Yajnavalkya, how many gods are there?'

'Three.'

'Yes, of course,' he said, 'but really, Yajnavalkya, how many gods are there?'

'Two.'

'Yes, of course,' he said, 'but really, Yajnavalkya, how many gods are there?'

'One and a half.'

'Yes, of course,' he said, 'but really, Yajnavalkya, how many gods are there?'

'One.'

Upanishads: Brihadaranyaka Upanishad, 3.9.1.

A great many Hindus favour one particular god or goddess, their *ishta-deva* or chosen one. Family tradition generally determines this, though some people may develop a special relationship with a deity, perhaps one who has answered their prayers at a time of need or who has come to them in a dream. But they also recognize and offer worship to many others. Similarly, in the stories where one god is pre-eminent, tales are told of his relationship with countless other deities. The divine – which Hindus may perceive as *brahma*n, or Devi, or Krishna, or another – manifests in many names and forms, and, in this sense, the many are an expression of the One. Yet both remain important. Hinduism is both polytheistic and monotheistic. Both the many and the One have a place within it, and within the common experience of most Hindus themselves.

Responses to the Divine Presence

How do Hindus respond to the divine in their midst? They respond by making offerings to deities and propitiating spirits, as we have seen, and in other ways, too. Most Hindus have a home shrine in their kitchen (this being the most pure place in the house) or in another room. There they have images and pictures of their chosen deities and of holy people. To these they may offer food, water, incense, and light each day (see illustration on p. 59). While some Hindus may also make regular visits to a nearby temple for *darshana*, most attend only at times of festivals

9. Mrs Pushpa Soni worshipping at the shrine in her Bombay home

(when they may also fast, eat special foods, visit relatives, and give presents).

The festive calendar varies throughout India, depending on local traditions, favoured deities, and the presence of sacred sites. Such places may become centres of attraction to pilgrims at certain times in the year – perhaps at the anniversary of the resident god or goddess, or in commemoration of a mythic or historical event. Probably the best known occasion is the *Kumbh Mela (mela* means 'fair') held every three years at pilgrimage centres on the banks of sacred rivers. Thousands of

Sacred Times and Hindu Festivals

There are many festivals celebrated in India, and they vary from region to region. Even the start of the New Year differs, for some falling in October and for others in April. The calendar which is used to work out festival dates is not like the Western Gregorian one. Instead it is lunar, with each of the twelve months having a dark and light half coinciding with the phases of the moon. Different lunar days are considered auspicious or inauspicious for the worship of particular deities, for activities such as fasting, travelling, and getting married. There is a right time for everything, and determining when is the job of the astrologer.

Because of the differences between the Hindu and Gregorian calendars it is impossible to give exact dates for festivals, although it is possible to give a rough guideline. Not all of them are celebrated by every Hindu – some have a special regional meaning; others are kept only by devotees of a particular deity. Some festivals are family-based; others are occasions when temple-visiting and pilgrimage are popular. Here is a list of some of the important festivals:

Divali, Deepavali (October/November): Festival of lights. Lasting several days, it is variously associated with the gods Rama and Krishna and the goddess Lakshmi. Small lamps are lit and presents are often given.

Makar Sankranti, Pongal, Lohri (January): *Makar Sankranti* means 'entry into Capricorn'. It traditionally marks the end of the harvest and is often celebrated with fireworks and sweets. It is celebrated as *Pongal* in Tamil Nadu, where rice is boiled and offered to the sun.

Shivaratri (February/March): Principal festival for *Shaiva* Hindus when offerings are made to Shiva and his praises are sung.

Holi (March): Festival often associated with the defeat of a demoness called Holika. Coloured powders or paint are often thrown in a spirit of merriment and mischief.

Ramnavmi (April): Celebration of the anniversary of the birth of Rama. The *Ramayana* is read.

Ratha Yatra (June/July): 'Car festival', when Lord Jagannath (a form of Krishna) is pulled through the streets in a huge chariot in Puri, Orissa (and also in Western cities where the Hare Krishna Movement is popular).

Raksha Bandhan (August): Festival which reinforces family relationships. Girls tie threads around their brothers' wrists in exchange for protection and a small gift.

Krishna Janamashtami (August/September): Principal festival for Krishna, celebrating his birth. The *Bhagavata Purana* is often read.

Onam (August/September): Harvest festival in Kerala, when traditional snake-boat races are held.

Ganesh Chaturthi (September): Festival celebrating the god Ganesha, particularly important among Maharastrians.

Navaratri, Durga Puja (September/October): Festival for the Goddess. *Navaratri* or 'nine nights' of folk dancing to worship Ambamata: celebrated by Gujaratis in India and abroad. Important in Bengal where elaborate images of Durga are created for the Goddess's worship.

Dashera, Dussehra (September/October): The 'tenth', the night following *Navaratri* when Rama's victory over Ravana is celebrated. In parts of north India, plays (*Ram-lila*) are performed which recount the story from the *Ramayana*.

In addition to annual festivals, there are some rituals which take place on a monthly or weekly basis, especially fasts to particular deities, such as the monthly *Ekadashi*, during which Krishna is petitioned, and the use of Friday to pray to the Goddess. Also important are fairs (*mela*), life-cycle rites (*samskara*), and national occasions such as *Vaisakhi* (a spring holiday celebrated on 13 April) and Republic Day (26 January).

holy men gather there, including the *Shankara-acharya*s, other religious leaders, and their ascetic followers (*sannyasis*). They are joined by millions of Indian pilgrims, many of whom make a once-in-a-lifetime visit to the *mela* to bathe, take *darshana* of the spiritual throng, and receive blessings.

The divine presence has elicited many different responses from Hindus.

We will conclude by looking briefly at two of these: honouring the deity in the temple, and serving the deity through communal religious life.

1. Madurai, a temple city

This ancient temple city in Tamil Nadu is more than just a great place of worship. Its temple architecture and sculpture are themselves a testimony to the way in which earlier generations of Hindus sought to serve and praise their sovereign deities. Originally centred on a royal palace and the figure of the king, Madurai came under the influence of a growing devotional movement which took hold in the south. A large and prestigious temple city grew up there at a time when temples were being sponsored and erected throughout the region by ruling dynasties (from the sixth to the ninth centuries CE). The present structure is from a later period and shares some of the same features as other south Indian temples, with towering gateways (*gopuram*), laid out on a square plan, with a large tank for ritual bathing, and two principal temples each containing an inner sanctum under a golden tower (*shikara*) with halls and an antechamber. The sacred centre in each is referred to as 'the cave within the mountain', and in them reside the divine guests – in one, Minakshi, the royal queen and warrior-turned-goddess, and, in the other, her husband, Sundareshvara (a form of Shiva, residing in a *linga*).

It is Minakshi, not her husband, who is the principal deity of Madurai and she is sometimes worshipped on her own, although the festive occasion of her marriage to Sundareshvara is celebrated annually by some 50,000 pilgrims. Each day in the public worship conducted by temple priests for the benefit of all, after being praised and showered with offerings, a portable image of Sundareshvara is brought ceremonially to the bedchamber of Minakshi, where the two deities are sung to and rocked in their swing before spending the night together behind closed doors.

On an ordinary day at the temple 20,000 to 25,000 visitors may pass through, attending the public *puja*, as well as performing their own

10. Minakshi temple in Madurai

devotions. They may also obtain the services of a priest to make offerings on their behalf and to recite the 108 names of the deity. These brahmin priests gain the right, purity, and power to serve Minakshi and Sundareshvara by virtue of being born into a particular caste and by undergoing rites of initiation and consecration. They serve the needs of the deities and are also the channels through which ordinary devotees make offerings and receive divine blessings.

2. ISKCON, a worshipping community

Such ordinary devotees may also respond to the divine presence by accepting the refuge or shelter of a guru, sometimes becoming involved in his or her *sampradaya*. In this last example, we will look at such a religious movement, one that grew up around A. C. Bhaktivedanta Swami, a Bengali *sannyasi* who left India at the age of 69 to spread awareness and love of Krishna in the West. The movement which he founded in 1966, the International Society for Krishna Consciousness (ISKCON), grew quickly before his death in 1977. It now has followers in India and other developing countries, as well as in the West.

Those who have met Hare Krishna devotees or bought their books may be familiar with two phrases which reflect their ideas about the divine and the human response to it. In the first, Krishna is referred to as 'the supreme personality of god-head', indicating that he is the ultimate divine person with whom devotees seek a relationship. In the other, 'back to god-head' (also the name of the Society's magazine), the desire of the devotee to return home to his or her eternal relationship with Krishna is expressed. From the writings of Bhaktivedanta Swami, particularly his commentaries on the *Bhagavad-gita* and *Bhagavata Purana* (known to devotees as *Srimad Bhagavatam*), devotees learn to see all their actions as opportunities for divine service. This extends beyond worship of Krishna in the temple to the private daily chanting of the Hare Krishna *mantra*, to singing the names of the Lord and preaching his glories, and to everyday labour during which his name should be repeatedly remembered.

Devotees repeat, as their founder did, the plea of the sixteenth-century Bengali saint, Chaitanya, that the name of Krishna should be spread in every town and village. To take this seriously means that devotees should not be content to respond to Krishna solely by improving their own spiritual discipline, but also by exposing others to Krishna and the path of devotional service (*bhakti yoga*). Invitations are extended to people to visit temples and take *darshana*, to attend lectures, buy books, join festival programmes, and eat *prashada*, food blessed by Krishna. Public worship, processions, and pilgrimages take the name and form of Krishna on to the streets of India's villages and the big cities of the West.

Like the widespread response to the miracle of Ganesha, such worship of Krishna is a global phenomenon, evidence that the presence of the divine in its Hindu forms now extends beyond India. The historical changes which paved the way for this development are the subject to which we now turn.

Chapter 6

Hinduism, Colonialism, and Modernity

For you I live, O Allah-Rama.

Show mercy to your slave, my lord.

. . . And if God only lives in mosques,

whose land lies in between?

Can Ram reside in images and pilgrims' stops?

In neither one has he been seen.

The east is the abode of Hari;

Allah's station's in the West.

But Rama and Rahim both lie within my heart,

and there alone is where to seek them.

As many women, men, that have been born:

they're all your forms.

Allah-Rama's little child, Kabir

knows that one as his guru and his pir.

This is part of a poem entitled 'Warnings' by the fifteenth-century *bhakti* poet, Kabir. He lived in north India at a time when it was under Mughal rule and when Islam was the religion of the rulers. His family, of the weaver's caste, had become Muslims, though their conversion may well have been more a matter of form than conviction. Kabir, at least, was disgusted by the outward practice of both Muslims and Hindus. He believed strongly that God – who was ultimately without form – manifested in the hearts of his devotees. Ritual practices, images, symbols, and buildings were all unnecessary.

Kabir was just one of a great many Indian mystical poets who wrote lovingly in praise of God while criticizing social injustices and religious formalities. From the sixth century CE in southern India to the eighteenth century in Bengal, such poetry was spoken, sung, and written, with some poets expressing love of Vishnu or Krishna, others of Shiva or Devi, and those like Kabir (and Nanak, the first of the Sikh gurus) love of the supreme One without name or form. From before the time of Kabir and Chaitanya, the religion of the Hindus developed in the context of foreign rule, first the Delhi Sultanate (1211–1526) and Mughal empire (1526–1757), then the British Raj. I have chosen Kabir as an illustration because his words show the influence of both the religion indigenous to India and the religion of the conquerors.

In another poem, Kabir announced, 'Saints, I see the world is mad'. He believed that Hindus and Muslims had lost sight of the truth and taken refuge in irrelevancies, even resorting to religious antagonism and violence. He described a situation that was to continue beyond the period of Muslim rule to later centuries when Christianity, rather than Islam, was the religion of the rulers. Although neither the Mughals nor the British actually imposed their religion on the Indians, in general both eyed Hindu beliefs and practices with suspicion and saw their own religion as superior. There were exceptions to this: the sixteenth-century Mughal emperor Akbar was known for his deep interest in and tolerance of those of other religions, and the eighteenth-century British administrators who studied Hindu scriptures acquired a positive image of the religion of early India.

In such a brief introduction to Hinduism it is not possible to give a detailed history of the events which surrounded the presence of the Arabs and Turks, then the Europeans in India (see the timeline for dates). What is of most importance here is the impact of such a presence on the religion of the Hindus, and it is to this that we will now turn, in particular to the effect of British colonialism.

The European Discovery of Hinduism

Europeans traded with India for spices and textiles as early as the classical and medieval periods, though perhaps the best known trader was the Portuguese Vasco da Gama who arrived on the Malabar coast at the end of the fifteenth century in search of 'Christians and spices'. These two motives are indicative of what was to follow in later centuries: the European desire to see India in its own Christian image and judge it accordingly, and to benefit from its riches – its goods and its culture.

The arrival of the Portuguese was followed in the sixteenth and seventeenth centuries by the Dutch, British, and French, all of whom established trading companies. Of these, it was the British who strengthened their commercial and administrative position and came eventually to dominate India politically. From their base in Madras, the British East India Company secured Bengal by military force in 1757 and made Warren Hastings Governor-General in 1772. His period of office marked the intervention of the British Government in Indian affairs. Hastings is remembered as an administrator, but he was also important for his patronage of Sanskrit scholarship.

In this period, a number of books by Europeans were published about India and its religion. Many repeated the themes of earlier travel writing in which popular religion was abhorred and Hindu ethical and philosophical doctrines approved (though not always properly understood). From the 1770s, significant scholarly progress was made by men in the employ of the East India Company, most notably by Charles Wilkins, with the first English translation of the *Bhagavad-gita* (1785), and William Jones, with his *Asiatick Researches* (from 1789) including his translation of the *Manusmriti*. Both Sanskrit scholars presented the Hindu religion in a positive light, showing its antiquity and stressing the themes within it that a Western audience could admire in their own terms. As

Warren Hastings wrote in his recommendation of Wilkins's *Bhagvat-Geeta*,

> Every instance which brings their [the inhabitants of India] real character home to observation will impress us with a more generous sense of feeling for their natural rights, and teach us to estimate them by the measure of our own. But such instances can only be obtained in their writings: and these will survive when the British dominion in India shall have long ceased to exist, and when the sources which it once yielded of wealth and power are lost to remembrance.

While the Hindu scriptures were being brought to a new audience by such scholars – 'orientalists' as they became known – a very different study of Indian religion was being undertaken by a rather unusual figure. Based in Madras and the Deccan rather than Bengal, a French Jesuit rather than a British administrator, Abbé Dubois toiled to collect information for a manuscript on *Hindu Manners, Customs, and Ceremonies*. Like Hastings, Wilkins, and Jones, he was aware of the ignorance of most Europeans and sought to rectify this with a detailed ethnographical account acquired through many years of intimate acquaintance with Hindus. He lived as they did, dressed like them, and gained their confidence. He was circumspect in avoiding 'any display of repugnance' towards their behaviour. His manuscript was translated into English (1815) and quickly became a resource for those Europeans eager to form an opinion of the religious culture of India.

Christianity and Neo-Hinduism

Abbé Dubois's account was full of colourful detail about the caste arrangements, brahminical lifestyle, and religious practices of south Indian Hinduism, yet his purpose was not to commend, but to inform. As a Jesuit, he was eager to promote Christianity and felt it was only possible to do this once one had a deep knowledge of Indian society and culture: 'It struck me that a faithful picture of the wickedness and incongruities of polytheism and idolatry would by its very ugliness help greatly to set off the beauties and perfections of Christianity.' Those of a more evangelical persuasion – like the anti-slavery campaigner William Wilberforce – disagreed and would have preferred the British administration in India to have been more proactive in outlawing such practices and promoting Christianity, but many of those in power were wary of antagonizing the population and provoking civil unrest.

Although the East India Company only formally lifted its ban on missionary activity in its territories in 1813, a few zealous Christians had settled before this. A key figure was William Carey, a Baptist who came to India in 1793. With no official backing or sponsorship, he spent several years with his family in bitter poverty, travelling through Bengal before setting up the Serampore Mission with two other missionaries. He learnt Bengali and Sanskrit, translating the Bible into Bengali in 1800. As a proselytizer, he was largely unsuccessful, however, since very few Bengalis embraced Christianity. Elsewhere, where Hindus did convert, it was not the hoped-for brahmins, but the powerless and disenfranchised lower castes and untouchables who made the change.

One Hindu brahmin who was known to the Serampore missionaries and was influenced by them was Ram Mohan Roy (1772–1833). With a command of Persian, Arabic, Greek, Latin, and English as well as Bengali and Sanskrit, and a knowledge of Islam and Christianity as well as his own Hindu religion, he was the first Indian to comment in print in English on the British, their religion, and its place in the Indian context. As a social reformer, he managed to outrage orthodox Hindus by writing against idolatry, *sati*, child-marriage, and caste, and in favour of education for women. And, as a Hindu with new ideas, he was praised and criticized in turn by Christians – praised for reading the New Testament, for his appreciation of the ethical teachings of Jesus, and his Unitarian sympathies, but criticized for his failure to accept Jesus as the son of God. Roy's reforming zeal was not confined to social issues. In 1828, he formed the Brahmo Samaj with like-minded friends in order to

11. An etching of *sati* from *India's Cries to British Humanity* by James Peggs, published in 1832

promote the reasoned, ethical monotheism which he believed to be rooted in the *Upanishads* and *Brahma Sutra*. Images of gods and goddesses and their worship was forbidden on Samaj premises. Looking back at this movement and the many writings of Ram Mohan Roy, it is possible to see the influence of both Islam and Christianity as well as *advaita vedanta* on his thought. Striking also is the way in which his ideas were disseminated. A truly modern Indian, he made use of all the novel means at his disposal, printing pamphlets, circulating newspapers, and petitioning for civil rights.

Hinduism on the Offensive

The reformist impulse of the Brahmo Samaj continued, particularly through the campaigning efforts of a later leader, Keshub Chandra Sen (1838–84), who pursued women's issues still further by calling for widow remarriage. Other nineteenth-century figures made similar pleas. Dayananda Saraswati (1824–83), who founded the Arya Samaj in 1875, stressed the Vedic religious partnership between men and women and the importance of women's education. He and others looked

Suttee or *Sati*?

As 'widow-burning', suttee was condemned by the British and French as inhumane. Accounts of it by travellers alerted compatriots back home in Europe to its horrors. The etching from the missionary account of James Peggs depicts two European observers turning away from the scene and aggressive Indians wielding swords and fanning the flames. The burning woman is presented as a passive, appealing victim.

Yet *sati* was not understood in this way by those Hindus who condoned it. *Sati* meant, in fact, 'a good woman', a devoted wife who chose to overcome death by becoming a goddess or *sati-mata*. Although the practice was not widespread, it certainly occurred with some regularity in parts of north India in the eighteenth century where it was considered an appropriate choice for high caste women whose husbands died before them. But while many orthodox Hindus supported it, there were others who despised it, most notably Ram Mohan Roy who campaigned vigorously for its abolition. The British, who were loath to interfere in Hindu religious affairs, were cautious, but eventually passed an Act in 1829 prohibiting it.

But it is not easy to legislate against popular beliefs and practices, and occasional instances of women's self-immolation continued. In 1987, in the village of Deorala in Rajasthan, a young wife named Roop Kanwar died on her husband's funeral pyre, and *sati* again became a contentious issue. Defended by her family, other local people, and many Hindu leaders, Roop's action was said to be her own choice. But many women in India asked, 'What woman would choose to die such a death?' Could this really have been a free choice, or was Roop pressurized into mounting the pyre? Pro-*sati* Hindus claimed that these critics were mere secularists, influenced by Western colonial

> animosity; those against *sati* denied that they were anti-Hindu,
> asserting only that they despised a practice which was oppres-
> sive of women and which, in fact, had no significant scriptural
> sanction.

back to the great debates of the *Upanishads* in which women had taken part.

The focus on 'women's uplift', as it was often called, was one aspect of the trend by orientalists and Hindu reformers to reclaim the Aryan past. The argument, as we saw in Chapter 1, rested upon acceptance of the idea of a former great civilization which had gradually been eroded over the centuries by popular religious practices and social customs such as 'superstitions', 'idol-worship', 'polytheism', and 'caste abuse'. This argument became central to the Hindu nationalist cause, and was repeated not only by the Arya Samaj, but by later campaigners and movements (including those active today). It met with its critics, however, who doubted the historical accuracy of the claim to an Aryan golden age and dismissed the divisiveness of favouring the Aryans above all other religious groups.

Many of the new Hindu initiatives of the nineteenth century were pervaded in some way or another by the influence of Western culture and Christian values. Where Hindu leaders did not positively endorse these, they reacted against them: the Arya Samaj, for example, reconverted low caste Hindus who had been drawn to Christianity. Many new groups mimicked the organizational and administrative practices and structures of British societies, and, like Ram Mohan Roy, they used the printed word as a means of spreading their ideas.

One Hindu figure less affected by the colonial situation in India was Ramakrishna (1836–86). From a poor brahmin family, he had become a

lic; not materialistic, rational, or scientific.
, as were the two people who later formed
New York in 1875. Madame Helena
Olcott began a movement with occult
Hindu and Buddhist thought – particularly
carnation. The Theosophical Society
est, but also took its message eastward,
882. Its exponents, particularly an English
t (who later became leader of the Indian
d the wonders of Hinduism, defending it
and evoking pride in their heritage among
anda and the Theosophical Society we see
fermented in the West, returned to India
re. Scholars of neo-Hinduism have referred
effect'.

e of this can be seen with Mohandas K.
ati Hindu nurtured in Vaishnavism and
he region of his birth, Gandhi went to

12. *Sati* handprints: A memorial to women immolated on the funeral pyres of their husbands

Vivekananda's Achievements

1880s	Member of the Brahmo Samaj
1881	Met Ramakrishna
1886	Death of Ramakrishna; Ramakrishna Order established
1886–92	Travelled as a *sannyasi* of the Ramakrishna Order. Decisive insights at Cape Comorin
1893	Attended the World Parliament of Religions in Chicago
1893–6	Lecture tour of US and brief visit to England. (Main topics of lectures: Hinduism, especially *advaita vedanta*; East–West understanding; Indian social conditions)
1894	First Vedanta Society founded in New York
1896	Returned to India
1897	Ramakrishna Mission founded in India. Periodicals started for the dissemination of Ramakrishna's teachings
1899	Brief return to America
1902	Death of Vivekananda

The Legacy of Sarada Devi

A religious organization for women – the Ramakrishna Sarada Math and Mission – was formally established in 1954 in her name. Now also active in South Africa and Australia, it has some twenty branches in India at which women may study and live. It offers initiation to women according to vows endorsed by the orthodox *Shankara-acharya* tradition. It is one of only a few movements which enable women to renounce the world and become *sannyasinis*.

priest of the
He developed
saw present
journey in w
of the *advait*
Muslim spiri
impressed n
Narendrana
was this dev
his guru's v
Sarada Dev
husband's

From In

Vivekanan
Hindu tea
century W
formed la
referred t
of Ameri
Christian

When Vi
his mess
they bel
Waldo
translat
Hindu
collecti
some
The 'tr
roman
imagi

The 'Pizza Effe

The pizza, originally
migrants to Americ
developed into what
tomatoes, cheese, an
fancy. Successful Itali
took with them the n
the homeland before
Italian. The export of
formation, subsequer
to by the scholar Agel

mythical, ritualistic, symb
They were spiritual seeker
the Theosophical Society i
Blavatsky and Colonel H. S
leanings and an interest in
the ideas of *karma* and rein
remained popular in the W
settling outside Madras in
woman named Annie Besa
National Congress), preach
against missionary criticism
Indian Hindus. With Viveka
how ideas about Hinduism,
only to influence Hindus th
to this process as the 'pizza

Probably the clearest examp
Gandhi (1869–1948). A Guja
exposed to the Jain ideas of

London in the 1880s to study law. Leaving sacred India and going to the land of the foreigners was a momentous step for which he was ejected from the mercantile *bania* caste (though later ritually reinstated). Once settled, he sought out people with whom he could share some of his cultural traditions – those free-thinkers who had taken up vegetarianism and theosophy. It was with them that he read the *Bhagavad-gita* for the first time, as well as Sir Edwin Arnold's *The Light of Asia* (on the Buddha) and the New Testament, most notably the Sermon on the Mount.

The *Bhagavad-gita* – which he read in English – was to influence Gandhi deeply throughout his life, fuelling his thinking on non-attachment and the way of action (*karma yoga*) which became important in his non-violent actions of resistance against the British and his campaign for Indian self-rule. Gandhi's return to his spiritual roots was not without critical reflection, however. He accepted the four social categories of *varna*, but rejected untouchability; he upheld the traditional 'Sita' role for women, but argued for their rights. A cornerstone of his principles was *satyagraha*, holding fast to the truth, on which his political action was built. The one truth which lay at the heart of everything issued forth in an ethical and non-violent force for good.

Like the other neo-Hindus discussed here, Gandhi was committed to social reform and the reshaping of modern India with reference to her valuable spiritual traditions. He too developed his ideas and actions as one of the colonized in the context of British rule, sometimes imitating, sometimes resisting, but always influenced by Western images of India and Hinduism. The views of neo-Hindus like Gandhi and the images of Western commentators invite us to reflect further on the nature of Hinduism and the many ways in which it has been lived out and understood. But before we do so, we shall investigate the modern challenges posed to it by two groups at the centre of calls for reform – women and untouchables or *dalits*.

Chapter 7

Challenges to Hinduism: Women and *Dalits*

In the mid-1970s and from 1980 until her assassination in 1984, India's prime minister was a woman, Indira Gandhi; in 1997, as I write this, a *dalit* or untouchable, K. R. Narayanan, holds the office of Indian president. Does their attainment of these positions suggest that women and untouchables have now achieved equality with other groups in Indian society? And, turning to religion, could a woman or a *dalit* be appointed *Shankara-acharya* (see Chapter 2), perhaps the most revered religious office within orthodox Hinduism?

These questions raise important issues regarding social and religious traditions in India. But are they related? Are social/ political affairs separate from religious ones? In thinking about Hinduism, is it appropriate to ignore the former? As this discussion will show, such a distinction would be artificial and unworkable. In India, caste and gender issues are not simply social matters demanding a secular response; they are underpinned by religious ideas and maintained by ritual customs and brahminical institutions. The very nature of Hinduism as a religion, even 'religion' itself, is challenged by this interrelationship. But we will return to this consideration in the final chapter. First, we must investigate what lies behind questions of caste and gender in Hindu thought, and the contemporary claims of their chief protagonists, *dalits* and women.

Caste and Gender: Who is a Hindu?

In earlier chapters I described the institutions of *varna* and *jati* and the important idea of *dharma*, order and duty, and its meaning for different social groups. As I explained, an important text which discussed these was the *Manusmriti*. Written chiefly with the interests of the brahmin community in mind, it nevertheless mentioned other groups, including low caste *sudras* and those outside the *varna* system which it referred to as *chandalas*. Both groups – and women, too – were prohibited from hearing the *Veda* and denied initiation into twice-born status (and the wearing of the sacred thread). Of *chandalas*, Manu was dismissive, referring to them as 'dog-cookers' to denote their lowly status and impurity, barring them from owning property, and consigning them to dwell outside the village and perform its most demeaning tasks (sweeping, working with leather, and removing excrement). The touch of such a person was polluting to one of a higher group and required ritual purification. Brahmins, the most pure of all, had most to fear from the presence of *chandalas,* even though they depended on them to carry out polluting tasks. *Chandalas* were seen as necessary but marginal to the village and its social and religious life.

Also polluting was a menstruating woman. Her touch would require a brahmin to bathe. High caste women, Manu said, should be under the protection of fathers, husbands, and then sons. They should never be independent, owing to their weak, fickle nature and the social consequences of allowing women to act outside male authority. A man must honour his wife, however, though he must also control her, by force if necessary, and keep her focused on her domestic duties. Bearing children – particularly sons – was her virtue. A good wife should serve even a bad husband as god. She should not leave him and, once widowed, she should not remarry. By Manu's time all women were prohibited from hearing the *Veda* and they were denied the opportunity of renouncing the world (*sannyasa*).

Manu's prescriptions were intended for the women of the twice-born classes, and were certainly of less importance for those of lower status. However, the norms and expectations arising from them (for example, submissiveness to the wishes of the husband and his family, tolerance of abuse, preference for sons, and restricted freedom) pervaded Hindu society, affecting how all women felt they should behave and how others viewed them. Women were not marginalized to the same extent as *chandalas*, but they had no direct access to religious scriptures and institutions or to spiritual progress and a relationship with the divine.

If that was the theory, what about the practice? There are few descriptive accounts available of Hindu life in India before the nineteenth century, so we know little of the actual experience of these two groups. We do know, however, that the *bhakti* movement was one which gave some people a significant opportunity for self-expression. Women poets like Antal, Akkamahadevi, and Mirabai, and low caste poets like Kabir and the leather-worker Ravidas showed that love of God was open to all people, irrespective of gender or caste, and that it could be expressed openly in one's mother tongue. Barred from hearing the Sanskrit *Veda* and from access to the religion of the twice-born, they discovered their own spiritual path, an intimate and direct relationship with their Lord.

It was not until the twentieth century, however, that large numbers of women and untouchables became involved in voicing their own views and shaping the debates on gender and caste.

The Women's Movement

As we saw in the last chapter, the situation of women and the problem of caste were considered to be important in the agenda of colonialists and neo-Hindu reformers because they were thought to be a mark of India's religious and social decline. From the 1880s, middle-class women became increasingly involved in professional life and the movement for

13. A woman worshipping at a Shiva *linga*, from the Manley *Ragamala*, painted *c*.1610 in Rajasthan

reform, though progress was slow and difficult. One of the most committed women of this period was Pandita Ramabai (1858–1922), who campaigned publicly for the education of child-widows, women's admission to medical colleges, and the training of teachers. She wrote *The High Caste Hindu Woman* in 1887 and founded a residential school for young widows in 1889. She came from a brahmin family, but her disenchantment with the lack of opportunities for women within the Hindu reform and revival movement contributed to her decision to convert to Christianity, for which she was ostracized by Bengali Hindus. She was joined by other women in her call for women's education, their argument being that, as 'mothers of the nation', women should be adequately trained. Sarojini Naidu (1879–1926), a future leader of the women's movement and Indian National Congress, said: 'Educate your women and the nation will take care of itself . . . the hand that rocks the cradle rules the world.' Women's involvement in nationalism grew with their calls for education, and both Annie Besant and Sarojini Naidu drew on the Hindu goddesses and women in Hindu mythology to provide role models for women and their involvement in political struggle.

This activism continued from the 1920s to Indian independence in 1947, during which time women joined with men in campaigns for civil disobedience organized by Gandhi in his pursuit of Indian self-rule. They fought to be allowed to participate in the salt march of 1930 to demonstrate against the salt tax imposed by the British, and were then made leaders of many of the groups set up to break the salt laws, boycott the use of foreign cloth, develop home industries, and arrange pickets and demonstrations. Many women were arrested for their participation in such actions.

Once the independence of India was achieved, women were once again able to focus on gaining equality and rights. They were hopeful that the new Government would enshrine these within the Constitution and a new Hindu Code Bill. Equality was indeed guaranteed in the Constitution of 1950, but their hopes regarding the raising of the age of consent and marriage, women's right to divorce, and changes to the laws on inheritance and dowry did not materialize in a new Bill (though some were later introduced in separate Acts).

It was not until the 1970s and 1980s, however, that campaigning for rights spread from the few, educated voices of politically aware women to the grassroots, with initiatives growing throughout the country for agitation *against* dowry and its abuse, domestic violence, rape, and *sati*, and *for* workers' rights for women, improvements to inheritance laws, environmental protection, and a common civil code. After several unsuccessful attempts, an all-India women's association had first been formed in 1917, but the 1970s and 1980s saw the coming of age of the movement for women with groups forming in cities, towns, and villages to deal with local concerns, and with women from all social and religious strata willing to speak and act publicly. The setting up in 1978 of *Manushi*, a journal for women by women (co-edited by Madhu Kishwar and Ruth Vanita), provided the opportunity to reappraise women's situation, their roles, images, and visions. In this, as in many other initiatives, women worked together, aware of their common interests as well as different starting points. They protested against the rise of communalism, in which the different religious and political agendas of Hindus, Muslims, and Sikhs came increasingly into conflict, and which threatened the efforts of the women's movement to make gains for all women irrespective of background.

Daughters, Dowry, and Sex Determination

Even before the composition of the *Manusmriti*, Vedic society was male-dominated with men heading the household and inheriting property. It was the *dharma* of women to give birth to sons: 'The birth of a girl, grant it elsewhere. Here grant a son.' (*Atharva Veda* 3, 23.) This idea persists, as this women's prayer shows: 'May houses be full of daughters-in-law but very few daughters; may they see the faces of grandsons and great-grandsons.' Many autobiographical accounts by

Indian women also confirm this sense that a daughter's birth is not always welcome. The failure to produce a son is often seen as a punishment for misconduct in a previous life, with unhappy consequences for the here and now. Not only are sons the ones who by tradition support the family and conduct rituals at the death of their parents, but they also bring wealth into the family at the time of marriage. Daughters, however, are a drain on the family's resources, as money and goods (dowry) have to be given by her parents to the groom and his family when they marry.

Dowry was prohibited in an Act of 1961, but what was once confined to higher caste communities is now a widespread and growing practice, with the costs of marrying a daughter rising annually. And, although both men and women claim to be against it, the practice continues. Of still greater concern is the abuse of wives which is associated with it. Demands are frequently made by husbands and in-laws for more money and goods after the marriage, and these are often violently enforced. Deaths occur increasingly. Young wives are murdered – usually by burning – so that a husband is free to remarry to obtain another dowry, and, not infrequently, women commit suicide because of incessant abuse: 'Girl dies of burns' (*The Hindu*, 16 February 1995); 'Housewife ends life after dowry harassment' (*The Deccan Herald*, 20 November 1994).

Since the end of the 1970s many women and men have campaigned actively against dowry in India and beyond. Some families have refused to participate in the giving or taking of dowry, an idea encouraged by a number of religious groups. The law on dowry in India was amended in 1983, and some abusers have since been imprisoned, but distinguishing between a kitchen accident and a dowry murder has proved difficult for the police and the courts.

Imagine the anxiety, then, of parents with daughters and no sons. How is the money to be raised for their dowries, and, once married, will they

14. A low caste woman by a Bombay building development

become the victims of such abuse? It is in the context of such fears that choosing the sex of one's children must seem tempting. For would-be-parents who can afford the amniocentesis test and an abortion if necessary, such sex-determination is possible. 'Abortions galore as sex tests flourish' ran a headline in *The Times of India* in 1986, and in Bombay in the same year research showed that, of 8,000 fetuses aborted following such a test, all but one were female.

What questions do these human rights abuses pose for Hinduism? Are they addressed by contemporary Hindu groups? How do such groups respond to the deep-seated bias towards sons within Hindu tradition? To what extent do Hindu women believe that their religion can be reformed to recognize their value and interests? Have some decided, like Pandita Ramabai, that traditional and neo-Hindu groups offer no hope and looked instead for spiritual alternatives, either in other religions or in new spiritual initiatives?

Untouchability and the Rise of *Dalit* Identity

Like abuse of women, crimes against untouchables are all too frequently reported in India's newspapers (cases exceed 10,000 a year). Those the Government designated 'Scheduled Castes' and Gandhi named *Harijans* (children of God), together with Indian tribal people, make up nearly one-fifth of the Indian population, most living in India's villages as landless agricultural labourers, with many bonded to those of higher castes. Despite their number, their equality with other Indians in the Constitution, and the Untouchability Offences Act of 1955, which was put in place to protect them, they are frequently the victims of violence, rape, and individual or mass murder, and continue to be denied their rights (to education, entry to temples, freedom of residence, and the use of wells). Government policies which have reserved them places in education and government service have enraged those higher caste Hindus who have to compete for places on merit, and widespread violence has often followed.

Ambedkar: What Path Freedom?

Legal and political recognition for untouchables and an informed collection of writings on all aspects of the position, history, culture, and politics of untouchability were the principal legacies of Dr B. R. Ambedkar (1891–1956). Unlike those reformers who spoke out against caste but, like Gandhi, hoped for a moral revolution within Hinduism which would enable untouchables to enjoy the same spiritual and social opportunities as other Hindus, Ambedkar was a radical who wanted to see change enshrined in law. He was also an untouchable, though an unusual one for his time. Following higher education at Columbia University, New York, and the London School of Economics, he returned to India and involvement in national politics, taking part in pre-independence negotiations with the British and, after 1947, assuming a leading role in the constitutional drafting committee.

His interests lay in what he referred to as the material and spiritual conversion of the untouchables, the former leading him to work for social democracy, rights for landless labourers, and the criminalization of offences against untouchables. In pressing for their spiritual conversion, Ambedkar first analyzed the contribution of Hindu teachings to the plight of untouchables. There was no equality in Hinduism, and no place for individual progress or judgement, he said. 'I tell you all very specifically, religion is for man and not man for religion. To get human treatment, convert yourselves . . . Convert for securing equality. Convert for getting liberty . . . Why do you remain in that religion which prohibits you from entering a temple . . . from drinking water from a public well? Why do you remain in that religion which insults you at every step?'

Having declared as early as 1935 his intention not to die a

Hindu, Ambedkar, with half a million followers, rejected his religious past and publicly embraced Buddhism in 1956, thus offering untouchables a new religious identity, one which accepted the existence of suffering yet taught a path to its cessation through individual effort.

Like women, the large untouchable minority is not a homogeneous group, but is divided by caste and language. Internal differences made joint action difficult, but, by the 1970s, a new and distinct identity was beginning to emerge from the activities of writers and small grassroots groups throughout India. Their focus was on their common situation as *dalits*, those who were 'broken', 'scattered', and 'oppressed'. Through the literature and performance of protest, newspapers and journals such as *The Dalit Voice*, local acts of resistance, and interventions by Scheduled Caste MPs in political debate, untouchables and tribal Indians began to act together and make their voices heard. Their leaders called for *dalits* to embrace secular humanism as a moral creed based on the present well-being of humanity, and to reject the divisive hierarchical laws and duties associated with orthodox Hinduism and the other-worldly focus of religion in general. *Dalit* thinking was 'counter-cultural', the objective being to claim an alternative history and identity not bound by the dominant ideology of brahminical Hinduism, but which might offer a way forward to a more just and open future. As the Gujarati *dalit* poet Neerav Patel wrote in 'Burning at Both the Ends',

> we can love each other
> if you can shed your orthodox skin.
> come and touch, we will make a new world –
> where there won't be any
> dust, dirt, poverty, injustice and oppression.

Religion and Protest

Many people in the modern *dalit* and women's movements have turned from Hindu to secular answers in the hope of attaining equality and justice. There were great hopes that, after Indian independence, the secular Government of India would effect change for both groups through the law. Such change has been disappointingly slow and, even when new Acts were brought in, they proved difficult to enforce against the weight of religious and social tradition and the force of vested interests.

Secularism has not been the only haven for oppressed groups, however. As we have seen, in the centuries before it became an option, women and low caste people found that the path of *bhakti* offered them self-esteem and an opportunity for liberation. Tantric and *Shaiva* movements were more accommodating than *Vaishnava* ones, particularly in the south, where the challenge to brahminical orthodoxy was strongest. Non-indigenous religions also had an appeal, particularly for those from the low castes. Kabir's family, as we saw in Chapter 6, had converted to Islam. In the nineteenth century some untouchables responded to the missionary pressures of Christianity (evoking a strong reaction from Hindu revivalist movements, which began their own campaigns of outreach to the low castes). Even today, around 80 per cent of India's Christians are from untouchable communities.

Embracing a new religious identity which offers equality and liberation, and denying the old with its inherent injustices, has been an important strategy for *dalits*. Some followed the lead of Ambedkar into Buddhism, and others became Sikhs. But these other religions have not always offered an adequate answer to their needs. Those who converted to Sikhism, for example, were referred to as *Mazhbi Sikhs*, and were clearly distinguished from those of higher castes. As a result, *dalits* have begun to form their own religious communities, reclaiming religious figures and symbols which they believe can affirm their humanity and liberate them from oppression. Different groups of Punjabi *dalits* have come to associate themselves with Valmiki (the renowned storyteller of the *Ramayana*) and to revere Ravidas (the untouchable *bhakti* poet), and religious organizations have grown up around them.

Inverting Hindu symbols and traditions as a form of protest is not new. For centuries in south India, those outside the top castes have asserted a subversive Dravidian, low caste identity by telling the *Ramayana* story with Ravana as hero and Rama (who signifies the north Indian, brahminical worldview) as villain. Rural women, too, as we saw in Chapter 4, have their own versions of the story which run counter to more orthodox renditions.

But women's religious protest has often been different to that of the *dalits* because of their situation within Hindu society, particularly within the family. They are separated from one another by their positions as daughter, daughter-in-law, mother, mother-in-law. Nevertheless, the songs they sing and stories they tell within the family often provide space to overturn the status quo, to complain and mock. And in their rituals, which do not require the presence of a brahmin, women are the experts.

Those neo-Hindu movements which have been established by and for women, such as the Order developed in memory of Sarada Devi, have often challenged women's place in the Hindu family by encouraging women to leave it and to live as students or renouncers. What is now known as the Brahma Kumari movement, founded by a man called Dada Lekhraj in the 1930s, came into conflict with the families of its early women members because it encouraged chastity and asexual love. Brahma Kumaris do not protest vocally against the sexual and physical abuse of women within the family, but they offer an alternative, seeking a gradual transformation of family relationships through *yoga* and abstention from alcohol and sex.

These examples show that religious protest by women and *dalits* has taken many forms, from the pursuit of religious and secular alternatives to remaining within a Hindu framework while seeking to reclaim its symbols, undermine its structures, or transform its traditions. To return to the question asked at the beginning of the chapter, it is still unlikely that either a woman or a *dalit* will be accepted in the role of *Shankara-acharya* in the near future, but the issue of spiritual and material equality is certainly on the agenda, not only with women and *dalits* themselves, but also with mainstream Hindu religious bodies. But this raises a difficult question about Hindu *dharma* as it is expressed in orthodox texts such as the *Manusmriti*. Can such equality be achieved without a radical transformation of Hindu teachings on purity and pollution, and on the nature and duty of women and untouchables? We shall come back to the question of Hindu *dharma* in the final chapter, but we turn now to a further challenge to Hindu identity – the movement of Hinduism beyond India.

Chapter 8

Crossing the Black Waters: Hinduism beyond India

While the boundaries of Hinduism have been challenged by the voices of low caste people and women's groups, their location and stability have also been called into question by the emigration of Hindus and the export of Hindu spirituality.

Those scholars who have sought to classify and typologize religions and their various dimensions have tended to see Hinduism as an *ethnic* religion, a religion of a particular people, and associated with their land or place. According to this view, a person was a Hindu by virtue of his or her birth within an Indian Hindu caste. Such a person, by tradition, was then subject to the *dharma* of his or her community, its rules and customs. The realm of *dharma*, the Hindu universe, was known as *bharat*, the land ritually purified by the brahmin and surrounded by *kala pani*, the black waters.

Historically, Buddhists, Christians, and Muslims have spread their religious ideas and practices by conversion and conquest. They are now found as majority populations in many different countries. Nearly all the world's Hindus, however, continue to live in the secular state of India, where they represent about 78 per cent of a population of 900 million, and Nepal, where Hinduism is the state religion and where 90 per cent

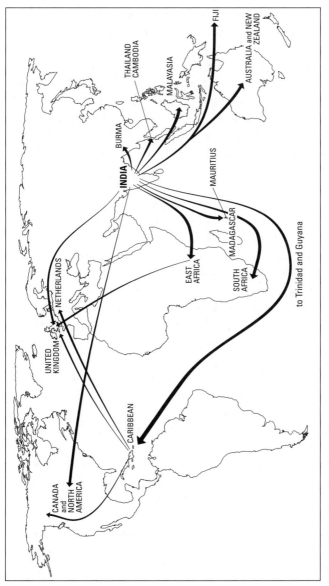

Map 2. Hindu Migrations from India

of Nepalese are Hindus. This seems to lend strong support to the idea that Hinduism is an ethnic religion rather than a universalizing religion with a message for all, regardless of birth and location.

However, throughout the history of *bharat*, the sacred land we now call India, there have been those, like Gandhi and Ambedkar, who have left her shores for education, trade, or a profession, to settle or to work and then return home. How have they justified and managed their journey and period of residence across the black waters? One instructive story is told by an anthropologist, Richard Burghart, in *Hinduism in Great Britain*:

In 1902 Madho Singh, Maharaja of Jaipur, was invited to London to attend the coronation of Edward VII. It was fitting that Madho Singh attend the ceremony, for Edward was Emperor of India and the Jaipur ruler owed him allegiance. Yet the Hindu king was filled with apprehension at the prospect of crossing the ocean and accepting British hospitality. To him, Great Britain was a remote, barbarous country, situated in the northwestern sector of the inauspicious 'Black Sea'. Madho Singh could not sustain his sacred person in such an alien environment. And such a journey would put his subjects at risk, for in the course of his coronation the people of Jaipur had been ritually constituted within the body of the king. Were Madho Singh to become personally defiled by his journey, his land and people would also become defiled. Thus Madho Singh faced a dilemma. He could travel to Great Britain, but only on condition that he did not leave India. He eventually found a way round his problem by chartering a ship, the S.S. *Olympia*, having the vessel cleansed throughout and ritually consecrated by the royal priest of Jaipur. Rice, dried fruit, vegetables, and water were brought on board, together with cows and fodder so that fresh milk could be supplied daily. Earth from the Sacred Land of the Hindus (*bharatavarsha*) and water from the Ganges were put in storage so that he could perform his daily ablutions and purify his alien surroundings. In this auspicious environment Madho Singh was safely conveyed to Britain.

As Burghart goes on to point out, however, Madho Singh was not the first Hindu to face this problem. In the early centuries CE brahmins travelled into south-east Asia (to what is now Cambodia, Thailand, and Bali) at the invitation of local rulers to consecrate their kingdoms. They remained, marrying local women, extending the ritual boundary of the sacred territory of *bharat*, and establishing aspects of brahminical culture such as their deities and scriptures. Today, in Thailand, the historical importance of the god Brahma is still witnessed in the Dheva Satarn temple in Bangkok and in royal ceremonies. The *Ramayana*, or *Ramakien* as it is known locally, remains significant in popular cultural performance. Despite such a heritage, these countries today are no little Indias, and those brahmins who continue to live and practise there are now fully Thai or Balinese in all but religious inheritance.

Quite different has been the movement of merchants to other nearby countries for business. The Chettyars, a Tamil banking community, extended their business to Burma, Malaya (now Malaysia), Mauritius, and other parts of southeast Asia. Additionally, strong trading links have existed for many centuries between western India and East Africa. Earlier this century Gujarati and Punjabi migrants (Sikhs and Muslims as well as Hindus), attracted by the opportunities available to work under the British administration on the new railroads and as small traders, set themselves up in the growing towns and cities of Kenya, Uganda, Tanganyika (now Tanzania), and Nyasaland (now Malawi).

The majority of these later migrants were merchants and artisans rather than brahmins. Initially, they were content to leave regular religious duties to their families back home. Later, when they became more settled and were joined by relatives, they began to establish social and religious institutions for mutual support, education, cultural activities, and religious nurture. Gurus and swamis crossed the seas to visit these communities and encourage their religious practices. They often consecrated new temples and held festivals and other devotional meetings.

Although the countries of East Africa, like India herself, were colonized by the British, Hindus and Indians of other religious persuasions travelled there freely in search of work and financial gain. They were able to maintain links with the homeland. Those indentured by the British and Dutch after the abolition of slavery in the mid-nineteenth century and transported to the plantations of Trinidad, British Guiana (now Guyana), Dutch Guiana (now Surinam), Fiji, Mauritius, and South Africa were not so fortunate. Although promised the possibility of return to India, few were able to do so, with most settling in their new countries and eventually gaining their independence and the right to acquire land. The Hindu communities which grew up in these countries developed quite differently from one another, depending on factors such as their ethnic and caste composition, their relative size compared to other local communities, the impact upon them of indigenous religious, social, and political institutions, and their ability to acquire power and status.

An informative study of one country in which indentured Indian Hindus settled is *Hindu Trinidad*. The author, Steven Vertovec, depicts the colourful devotional life of the Hindus, describing particularly the musical renditions of the *Ramayana* which were popular in the 1960s and the grand, week-long *yajnas* (sacrificial rites) which were sponsored by families made newly rich in the oil boom of the 1970s and 1980s. He also mentions the brahmins who migrated with the indentured labourers to serve their religious needs, and the way in which regional and family traditions such as the worship of Kali often gave way to rituals endorsed by the brahmins. He ends with the demands of young Hindus for a vigorous and confident Hindu identity which might compete successfully with that of other aspiring groups in Trinidad.

With indentured Hindus arriving from 1845, Hinduism in Trinidad has now been establishing itself for over 150 years. The arrival of Hindus has been a more recent phenomenon in Britain, North America, and Australasia, where differing colonial traditions and immigration policies have led to variable patterns of settlement and community type. If we compare the Hindu populations of Britain and the United States, for example, we find that settlement began earlier in the former as a result of Britain's colonial relationship with India. The majority of Hindus, as British passport-holders, arrived in Britain from East Africa in the 1960s and early 1970s following the impact of nation-building policies in the newly independent states. Hindus in the USA, however, came directly from India as professionals, entering to take up jobs in healthcare, education, and business. Hindus in the West in general have achieved a very high educational level and good standard of living, though sadly many have also experienced racial discrimination and racism.

Interesting issues are raised concerning the nature of Hinduism as a religion by the presence of Hindu communities outside India (Hindus were resident in 68 countries by 1980). Clearly, Hindus have shown themselves to be resourceful and flexible people able to live, work, and create communities in many, quite different settings. The presence of a Hindu diaspora suggests that Hindus have been prepared to contravene, or at least to reinterpret, the brahminical injunction set out in the *Manusmriti* against crossing the black waters.

Although this does not counter the claim that Hinduism is best described as an ethnic religion – as most migrant Hindus have retained the practice of caste marriages and have not sought to widen the definition of who is a Hindu – it does invite scholars to review ideas about where and how Hinduism may be practised. The foundation of temples and the migration of brahmins able to carry out life-cycle rites, *yajna*, and *puja* have allowed Hindus to establish sacred spaces and perform the necessary ritual activities outside India. Does this represent an extension of the sacred territory of *bharat*, as we saw in the cases of Madho Singh and the early Brahmin migrants to south-east Asia? But what about those religious organizations, in many countries, which have been founded, managed, and led by enthusiastic and skilful lay persons who have raised funds, purchased property, organized festivals,

Diaspora

The concept of diaspora originally referred to those Jews who lived outside Judaea. In Judaism it is linked to the idea of exile. Today it is used very generally of other peoples living outside their land of origin, though their reasons for doing so may vary. Some may be refugees who have been forced to leave their homes; others may be migrants who have chosen to move for economic reasons. Hindu communities outside India have been composed of people with many different motives for leaving India.

youth and women's groups, the visits of spiritual leaders, and the employment of brahmins? Although such lay people have generally been the facilitators rather than the officiants of public religious life, at times they have conducted worship and served the deities directly, showing that the desire to live the devotional life has sometimes been considered more important than orthodox brahminical practice. As we saw in Chapters 5 and 7, the *bhakti* tradition within Hinduism offers the precedent and context for this. We might say that these Hindus have been inspired more by the spirit than the letter of their religion.

In countries outside India, temples (*mandir*) have often been fashioned from converted premises, from schools, deconsecrated churches, homes, even factories. As Hindu communities have grown wealthier they have opened purpose-built temples, designed either according to local styles or in imitation of those in India. In August 1995, the local population of the north London suburb of Neasden, with many thousands of Hindu devotees and invited guests, saw the opening of what *Reader's Digest* magazine chose to describe as the 'Eighth Wonder of the World', 'London's answer to the Taj Mahal'. Built from natural materials to Hindu scriptural specifications, and erected entirely by

Hindus Outside India: Population Statistics

Hindus constitute approximately 15 per cent of the world's population. However, there are no precise figures for the numbers of Hindus living outside India. One reason for this is that many countries do not keep statistics for religious adherence. The figures given below were for 1980 and were published in the *World Christian Encyclopedia* in which estimates were given for people of all religions, country by country.

Country	Number of Hindus	% of population
India	547,123,500	78.8
Nepal	12,757,430	89.6
Bangladesh	10,770,000	12.7
Sri Lanka	2,474,400	16.0
Pakistan	1,078,400	1.3
Indonesia	3,250,000	2.3
Malaysia	1,035,800	7.4
Fiji	259,700	40.9
Mauritius	446,700	46.0
South Africa	565,000	2.0
Kenya	80,000	below 1
Tanzania	19,000	below 1
Trinidad and Tobago	268,700	25.3
Guyana	304,150	34.4
Great Britain	380,000	below 1
Canada	45,000	below 1
United States	500,000	below 1

These estimates provide a snapshot of the world Hindu population at one point in time. But further information helps to contextualize them. For example, the Hindu population of what are now Bangladesh and Pakistan was much higher before the partition of India in 1947.

Several African countries are mentioned above, but not Uganda, despite the fact that many Hindus migrated there earlier this century. As late as 1970, there were some 65,000 Hindus living there, but every one of them was expelled a few years later by Idi Amin. In the late 1990s, some Hindus have returned there to live and work.

The estimates for North America are now out of date as Hindus have continued to enter as professional immigrants. There are also small Hindu populations in countries not mentioned here – Singapore, Australia, New Zealand, Thailand, and the Netherlands.

voluntary labour, the Shri Swaminarayan Mandir was the first traditional Hindu temple to be built in Europe. It is used for the regular worship and meetings of the Swaminarayan Hindu Mission, a Gujarati Hindu movement or *sampradaya* headed by a popular Indian guru called Pramukh Swami Maharaj. It is at least as important, however, as a tourist venue. Approached through rows of ordinary terraced housing and set back from one of London's busiest roads, it represents Hinduism in all its grandeur to non-Hindus, and shows what can be achieved by devotional service to God. As well as a tour round the magnificent temple with its marble, limestone, and teak carvings, the visitor can expect to see a video showing its construction and an exhibition of the Hindu heritage. On the other side of the road they will see the Swaminarayan School, one of only two Hindu day schools in the United Kingdom.

The Bochasanwasi Akshar Purushottam Sanstha, of which the

15. A postcard depicting the Shri Swaminarayan Hindu Mandir in Neasden

Swaminarayan Hindu Mission is the British branch, is the fastest-growing religious movement among Gujarati Hindus world-wide. With a network of 370 temples and several hundred thousand followers, it has held important cultural festivals in East Africa, Britain, and the USA, as well as in India. It is a devotional movement in the theological tradition of Ramanuja, in which followers worship a deity known as Swaminarayan as their supreme Lord. It provides single-sex educational and spiritual programmes for children, young people, and those in older age groups. It holds mass rallies and engages actively in voluntary work in all the countries in which it has a presence. It is just one of a number of popular *sampradayas* or sectarian groups operating within the Hindu diaspora.

Some of these movements remain almost exclusively 'Indian', though their membership includes those who are second-, third-, even fourth-generation Indian Americans, Indo-Caribbeans, British Indians, and African Indians. However, other global Hindu movements have a mixed membership, comprised of Indian Hindus *and* those from other ethnic backgrounds. They have a spiritual message which offers Hindu ideas and practices to those who were not born or nurtured as Hindus. We witnessed the rise of this message in Chapter 6 with the initiative of Vivekananda. The Vedanta Society he started in America now has both Indian and non-Indian members. ISKCON, the Shaiva Siddhanta Church, and the Sai Baba Fellowship have similar broad appeal, but there are other movements in which the following has been drawn almost exclusively from among Westerners: the American Self-Realization Fellowship founded by Yogananda Paramahamsa; Transcendental Meditation (which excited the interest of the Beatles in the late 1960s); Swami Muktananda's Siddha Yoga; the Neo-Sannyas programme of Bhagwan Rajneesh (also known as Osho); Mataji Nirmala Devi's Sahaja Yoga; and Iyengar Yoga. All of these, along with the mixed membership groups, recognize the interest of Westerners in aspects of Hindu spirituality, particularly in the chanting of *mantras*, *kundalini* meditation, *hatha yoga*, belief in reincarnation, and vegetarianism. Their presence in the West has been timely, helping to fill a spiritual vacuum and to offer ideas and practices to those seeking alternatives to Western religions and secularism.

This trend has sparked debate among Hindus about the nature of Hinduism and its boundaries. Are movements which offer only selected aspects of Hindu spirituality and make no reference to the Hindu social world authentically Hindu? Have Hindu ideas and practices been transformed beyond recognition in the process? Are members of such groups 'Hindus', or can a Hindu identity only be claimed by one born into an Indian or Indian-diaspora family? I will come back to these questions in the concluding chapter.

Without doubt, the role of the guru has been important in most of these contemporary movements, regardless of their membership. These gurus have been the focus for devotion, the mediators of tradition in what has often seemed to be the alien environment of the West, and the source of authority for those seeking knowledge or guidance. Some have offered systems of spiritual discipline requiring considerable effort and commitment; others have offered the repetition of a simple *mantra* or a short act of worship as the focus for happiness or self-realization. Some have been controversial and colourful characters, while others have been quietly charismatic. All have shown an astute awareness of the special demands posed by the Western context.

Gurus have not been the only individuals to have a role in the reproduction of Hinduism outside India, however. Within the Indian Hindu diaspora, family members, particularly women, have been of great significance in communicating Hinduism to the next generation. Temples establish classes to teach community languages, and *sampradayas* form youth groups to enhance children's knowledge of scripture and doctrine, but it is in the home that children learn their first religious lessons. There they are told stories about the gods and goddesses by their elders, or they read them in comic books or watch the video versions. They learn about Hindu festivals such as *Divali*, *Mahashivaratri*, *Durga Puja*, *Pongal*, and *Janamashtami*, getting to know the family traditions associated with each. Like young children in India, they also learn, by participation and imitation, how to perform *puja* at the home shrine and how to keep fasts. Like Madhur Jaffrey (see Chapter 4), some of them play-act Hindu stories or rituals, and young girls in particular may have real roles to perform as handmaidens of the Goddess in ceremonies associated with her worship. However, these children will not have the same experience as those in India of having Hindu ethical, social, and cultural traditions present in the world around them as, in most of the countries to which they have migrated, Hindus live as minorities. In some countries their religion has been tolerated but given little if any recognition in the media or in state education; in other countries, multiculturalist policies have operated giving Hindus a limited opportunity, along with other religious communities, to have their voices heard and their religion represented.

A tension arises in the Hindu diaspora, as indeed it does in India,

16. A procession, *Ratha Yatra*, in Trafalgar Square, organized by ISKCON

between two important requirements. One is the need to create a
strong, unified Hindu identity which can be articulated publicly and
compared to the other major world religions. The other is the desire of
many to stress the openness of Hinduism towards other religions and
the diversity of paths within it. The Vishwa Hindu Parishad supports the
first of these positions and is active around the world in promoting
Hindutva or 'Hindu-ness' and a sense of pride among Hindus. A number
of Hindu scholars, writers, and women's groups outside India have put
forward the opposing view, of religious and cultural difference, arguing
that the idea of Hindu unity is both ahistorical and unhelpful in enabling

Hindus to live positively with people of other religions and even with those in their own faith community who have differing perspectives.

There is no single version of Hinduism operating among Hindus in diaspora. Hindus of many castes and sects and from many parts of India have migrated, taking with them traditions that were familiar to them back home. They have also been influenced in the reproduction of their religious practices and beliefs by the place in which they have settled and its particular social and religious character. However, while developing their own local communities, they have remained in touch with Hindus world-wide, through kin, caste, and sectarian links, through newspapers and magazines circulated globally by Hindu groups and caste associations, and recently through Internet web sites and e-mail. These national and global networks have been instrumental in keeping Hindus informed of news and events and in transmitting ideas.

Hinduism Today is a monthly newspaper published in multiple regional editions (and archived on the Internet) for Hindus around the world. It is advertised as 'The Hindu Family Newspaper Affirming the Dharma and Recording the Modern History of Nearly a Billion Members of a Global Religion in Renaissance'.

It features articles on Hindu concepts, practices, traditions, and figures, and stories about Hindus in different countries. In its regional issues it also carries advertisements and notices of relevance to local Hindus. In an issue from April 1993, for example, readers were informed about several subjects of importance to Hindus everywhere, including a meeting of Hindu leaders about the Rama temple site in Ayodhya and a new sourcebook to help in the religious nurture of *Shaiva* Hindus. A century after the World Parliament of Religions in Chicago, Swami Vivekananda's achievements were celebrated with reflections from Hindus in the USA, Malaysia, and India. There were also general articles which provided information for the educational benefit of Hindu readers on the world's tribal peoples and on world religions. There were letters and book reviews, and readers were invited to make donations to fund the building of a temple in Hawaii. The edition ended with an illustrated article entitled 'Ramayana Animated' about a new Japanese film version of the famous story of Rama and Sita.

As the contents of Hinduism Today show, Hinduism in and beyond India is subject to both the continuity of its traditions and religious change. New concerns arise, such as the ethical issues surrounding reproduction and genetic engineering, and new contexts demand a fresh approach. The presence of Hinduism as a religion alongside others requires Hindus to think about and articulate what is important to them in ways which can be understood by outsiders. Yet the challenge of passing down what is sacred to new generations of insiders remains ever-pressing, as the words of this first-generation British Hindu woman show:

> Well, my parents were born and brought up in India so their life was different. I have many roles to fulfil, not just as a mother, but as a working wife, while my mother and grandmother only had one life, that of a housewife bringing up the family. I have tried my best to transmit my own culture and religion to my children because in this country they couldn't get this religious experience or culture in the outside world. My mother and grandmother didn't have to face this because at home [in India] children picked up religion. You were born and brought up with it. It was everywhere. My children were born in one environment, but they were facing a very different one outside the home. I'm not sure if I've been successful, but I think I've done my best.

Chapter 9
Hindu *Dharma*, Hinduism, and Hinduisms

17. A Bombay street scene

What do you see when you look at this picture? A cow? But what does that mean to you? A farm animal (in this case, out of place in a busy city street), source of meat and milk, leather and manure? A European observer might also think of the cow's possible association with heart disease and BSE, Mad Cow Disease. But an Indian viewer, while noting this ordinary cow, might go beyond it to see a sacred symbol, divine mother of all, in whose dung the goddess of prosperity resides. What you see depends on your standpoint. A cow signifies something different to Hindus and non-Hindus; but even within Hinduism her meaning differs depending on whether you are a brahmin or a leather worker, one who milks her or uses her products for fuel and cooking.

Hinduism is a bit like this, too. Outsiders and insiders see Hinduism differently, and those who are inside don't always think alike, as we have seen in previous chapters. It would be convenient to offer a simple definition of Hinduism or to categorize it neatly, but it refuses such treatment. To say a cow is an animal or Hinduism a religion tells us very little indeed. What type of animal? What type of religion? And what about their symbolic significance among Hindus?

I shall start this final investigation of Hinduism, the meaning of which I have so far taken as self-evident, by considering what it means to call it a religion. After that, I will look at how Hindus and visitors to India have viewed it, and will examine its derivation and changing meaning. But will it do to see Hinduism as a single system, or is it like the divine in India, both one and many? At that point, I will introduce a metaphor which might help us to think about Hinduism's diverse character and the important part played by power in its structure. To end, I will return to the cow and her relationship with Hinduism past and present in order to show how the meaning of 'Hinduism' is a matter of constant negotiation.

Defining Hinduism

To call Hinduism a religion raises the question, 'What is a religion?' The term 'religion' is Western in origin. It comes from Latin and originally meant the bond between people and their gods. In the study of religions, the principal example has been Christianity. By extension, 'other religions' have been those systems which have been judged to be analogous to Christianity, principally Judaism and Islam, both of which are Western and related historically to Christianity, but also Eastern systems such as Buddhism and Hinduism. Some of the key characteristics of Christianity against which 'other' religions have been compared and contrasted have been belief in a transcendent God, a founder, scripture, priests, an institution or church, and various dimensions such as belief, ethics, myth, and ritual.

Comparing Hinduism to Christianity, we see that it does indeed have a God – one ultimate reality and many gods and goddesses, in fact. But it has no founder, a multitude of scriptures rather than one book, brahmins but no priests in the Christian sense, and no central institution like a church. Ritual, myth, and ethics are important, but belief is of less significance, there being no core creed and few common teachings. But there might also be things intrinsic to Hinduism that just don't show up in a comparison with Christianity. For example, Hinduism extends into the complex socio-religious system of caste and the varied popular practices which, in Christian terms, constitute magic and superstition rather than religion. So, if Hinduism is a religion at all, it is a rather different one to Christianity, if the latter is to be the benchmark for religion. We may look for books on Hinduism in the 'Religion' section of libraries and bookshops, but we would be advised to try a few other sections as well.

One modern Hindu philosopher, Sarvepalli Radhakrishnan, declared Hinduism to be 'a way of life'. By doing so, he made the point that it was not something separate from society and politics, from making money, sex, and love, and getting an education. And, like other modern Hindus, he suggested that the closest term to be found within Indian thought and practice was Hindu *dharma*, the law, order, truth, and duties of the Hindu people.

This raises other questions. Whose *dharma* was intended? What does the term 'Hindu' mean? Unlike the term 'Hinduism', which was used first in the early nineteenth century by orientalist scholars to signify the religion of the 'Hindoos', the term 'Hindu' was of earlier derivation. It had been used by incomers to India, particularly Persians and Turks, to denote those people living around the river Indus in the north and, later on, all the people beyond the Indus, the entire population of India. By that token, Buddhists and Jains, Dravidians and Aryans were all included. The term when used by incomers had no obvious religious significance, referring only to a geographically defined group containing immense internal diversity of language and custom. Later, indigenous Indians began to use the term, too, though only in order to distinguish themselves from the Mughals and Europeans. Still it had no religious intention, rather an ethnic or national meaning.

But the meaning of 'Hindu' began to change. With the discovery by the British of Vedic scriptures and the brahmin class and culture, it began to be invested with religious significance (on the principal of it being analogous to the term 'Christian'). 'Hindoo' and, later, 'Hinduism' began to be identified with the religious traditions of the Aryan people, and this identification began also to be made by Indian reformers, though the idea of peoplehood and nation continued to be important in the light of calls for Indian self-rule.

Among scholars of religion the meaning and validity of 'Hinduism' has been much discussed as knowledge of its origins has grown. But more than anything, it is awareness of the internal complexity of 'Hinduism' which has called the term into question. Not only does it comprise the major divisions of Vaishnavism, Shaivism, and Shaktism, but it also offers a variety of different philosophical approaches, thousands of deities and their associated mythology and iconography, and innumerable ritual practices. It contains within it brahminism, which is often referred to as the orthodox or mainstream movement within Hinduism, as well as 'Hindu' challenges to brahminism, like those we examined in Chapter 7. And then there are the village traditions which extend beyond brahminism to pragmatic, magical, and animist practices. Nowadays, when scholars refer to 'Hinduism', they include all of these movements, traditions, beliefs, and practices. This explains the attraction of the other term mentioned in this chapter's title, 'hinduisms'. There do indeed seem to be many hinduisms rather than one Hinduism. But this invites further questions. Are they not related? If they are, what is the link?

The question of the relationship between the various religious movements and traditions, beliefs, and practices in India is difficult. Various non-Hindu and Hindu commentators have identified possible links, particularly the caste system, the authority of the *Veda*, the concept of *dharma*, and Aryan identity. Others have hotly denied the validity of such claims. If we were now to look back over the contents of this book at the interlocking themes, we would see that all those mentioned above, plus the popular narrative traditions of the *Ramayana*, reverence for the *Bhagavad-gita*, the presence of the divine in many names and forms, the place of the guru, and the sacred land of India, might also constitute defining features. There seem to be family resemblances between the various parts, but these resemblances are not always the same, just as grandparents, parents, siblings, aunts, uncles, and cousins may not all have 'the family nose', but may resemble one another in many different ways, some physical, some in terms of personality or attributes.

Pushing the family metaphor further, like relatives within a family, the various hinduisms exist in tension with one another, some being more alike than others, some being in fierce disagreement with one another. Although Buddhism and Jainism were traditionally seen as heterodox systems and, later, the incoming religions of Islam and Christianity were also seen by Hindus as categorically distinct, this does not mean that all the movements, schools, and traditions within the family of Hinduism were equally accepted by all. There are innumerable accounts of great contests between exponents of different branches of the *vedanta* school, and between those who followed different deities or gurus. And we have seen how rebellious *bhakti* poets and marginal groups criticized and challenged conservative, patriarchal brahmin elders and their social and ritual dominance.

The human metaphors of the family and family resemblance are not just a convenient way of holding together the different hinduisms or related aspects of Hinduism. They also help us to see the importance of power within it. It is all too easy to ignore this factor in thinking about religion, particularly today when spirituality rather than other elements of religion is so often stressed. Many Hindu writers have made this point. As *dharma* or 'a way of life', Hinduism is related to what Westerners refer to as 'secular' concerns, to economic, political, and social matters. In India, debates about religious identity are not just about religion, but neither are they just political or social debates in a religious guise. Just as family members try to make their voices heard, even to get the upper hand in day-to-day disputes, so Hindu individuals and groups struggle by whatever means to assert their beliefs and commitments, their caste interests, and sectarian viewpoints.

Dynamic Symbols: the Cow and Hinduism

This brings me to the final stage in this investigation of Hinduism – an assessment of what it has meant for modern Hindus and how they have used the term. The cow is my assistant in this, as her destiny as a symbol has been similar to that of Hinduism itself.

Even before the modern period, the cow was associated with several ideas: *ahimsa* or non-injury; purity and purification; goodness; and motherhood, in nurturing and providing not only for her calf but for all. In the Vedic period she was sometimes offered in sacrifice, but later it became an offence to eat her. In the *Mahabharata* and *Manusmriti*, she was associated with Shri, the goddess of prosperity, her products were considered to be pure and good, and she was to be revered as a great mother and provider. Both cows and women were referred to as goddesses, though the cow seems to have had a higher status because of her purity and value as a resource.

In the nineteenth century, her significance took a new turn. One of the things which distinguished the indigenous Indians or Hindus from incomers was their reverence for the cow and commitment to keeping her from harm. Sacrificing her or eating her, as Muslims and Christians were prone to do, was abhorrent to caste Hindus, and, in the context of a rise in religious self-consciousness among reforming groups, protection of the cow became a symbol for Hindu identity. The cow, like the Hindu woman, was identified as mother of the nation. Dayananda Saraswati of the Arya Samaj and Gandhi both wrote about the national importance of protecting the cow, and local societies were established throughout India to engage ordinary Hindus in looking after this great symbol.

There is no doubt that the importance given to the cow puzzled those outsiders who knew little about Hinduism. Arguments took place among Western scholars about whether the status of the cow in India could be justified on economic grounds. What they failed to appreciate was her symbolic value. She was both religiously *and* economically important. But the cow's place in Hinduism was questioned by insiders, too, as a patriarchal symbol and one with dubious implications for untouchables whose lowly status was reinforced by her representation of purity.

What can we learn about the destiny of Hinduism in the modern period from this extended illustration? What I have tried to show is how the idea of the cow came to have such significance for Hindus in the context of British India, becoming a focus for religious, political, and scholarly discussion and negotiation. The idea of 'Hinduism' only came to the fore in the modern period, but, like the symbol of the cow, it had its antecedents in the scriptures, practices, concepts, and institutions of earlier times. The phrase *sanatana dharma*, eternal tradition, used often by Hindus to describe their religion, implies antiquity, but its usage is modern.

The socio-religious traditions of the Hindus have endured for several millennia, and were clearly not an invention of the modern period. However, the particular interpretations given to them by orientalists, reformers, nationalists, the women's movement, and the *dalit* liberationists – to name just a few – have led to the creation of 'Hinduism' and the modern debate about its nature.

So, the cow as a symbol for the nation and Hinduism as a type of religion are modern ideas in India. The former has less relevance in an independent India, but the latter is still evolving. Neo-Hindu movements, for example, have changed the face of Hinduism, bringing social reform and Hindu spirituality to the fore. A moral imperative for the future of Hinduism, according to many Hindus, is its need to transform itself in order to be more open to marginal groups: Arvind Sharma's discussion of *karma* and caste (see Chapter 3) is a response to this. The invitation made by religious nationalists to a *dalit* to lay the foundation stone for the planned temple to Rama in Ayodhya, and the acceptance of women renouncers in some modern movements are further examples. Such trends run counter to traditional teachings, but illustrate that religious change is as much a part of Hinduism as the continuity of tradition which we witnessed in the early chapters of this book.

Ideas about the nature of Hinduism are also evolving within the debate about Hindu nationalism. India is formally a secular country, in which Hindus (by which I mean those who are not Muslims, Buddhists, Christians, etc.) are in the majority. Yet, as we have seen, the idea of the sacred land of India, her people and, by extension, the nation, are central to discussions about Hinduism. Claims and counter-claims about the early Indian Aryans and Dravidians, about unity and diversity within Hinduism, and the multi-religious history of India all contribute to the debate about whether Hinduism can and should become the national religion or whether India should continue to endorse and celebrate its religious plurality.

And, finally, what about the idea of Hinduism as a global religion? Although most Hindus continue to live in India, there are Hindu communities in most continents, making Hinduism a world religion. This is supported further by the relatively recent practice of taking the message of Hindu spirituality to non-Hindus. Whether the neo-Hindu movements which have done so are properly 'Hindu' is still being debated, but the practice has helped the spread of Hindu ideas. Even the cow has found a place in global Hindu spirituality. She remains relevant as a symbol of non-violence, but in a new context of ecological awareness, widespread vegetarianism, and a commitment to the integrity of all creation.

'Hinduism' defies our desire to define and categorize it. It is *both* a dynamic phenomenon of the modern world, evolving from the combined imaginations of many individuals and groups, Hindu and non-Hindu, *and* the sum of its many parts – its traditions, myths, institutions, rituals, and ideas – its many hinduisms. It has the power and diversity to capture the imaginations of Hindus and non-Hindus alike, and the capacity to challenge all preconceived ideas about what a religion is.

Appendix
The Six Philosophical Systems (*Darshana*)

The *Vedanta* system is one of six orthodox (*astika*) perspectives or systems (*darshana*) commonly identified in Hindu thought. Each has a *Sutra* text and commentaries which explain and interpret it. The Western distinction between philosophy and theology has little relevance for understanding the *darshanas*. They contain logic, analysis, and scriptural exegesis, and are often directed to the liberation or salvation of the self.

1. *Samkhya*: This dualistic and atheistic perspective focuses upon the distinctive nature of *purusha*, self or spirit, and *prakriti*, matter.

2. *Yoga*: The *yoga-darshana* builds on the dualism of *samkhya* but focuses on the spiritual discipline required for the self to attain liberation.

3. *Mimamsa*: Focusing on *dharma*, right action, this is a system of Vedic exegesis.

4. *Vedanta*: Also an exegetical system, *Vedanta* refers to the 'end of the *Veda*', particularly the Upanishadic teaching on ultimate reality (*brahman*).

5. *Nyaya*: A system of logic, leading to liberation.

6. *Vaisheshika*: A system of atomistic analysis of the categories of *dharma* and their constituent elements.

Timeline

Before Christian Era (BCE)

2500–1800	Indus valley period
1500–500	Vedic period; composition of Vedic texts (*Samhitas*, *Brahmanas*, *Aranyakas*, *Upanishads*)
566–486	Traditional dates for the life of the Buddha
500–100 CE	Composition of *Mahabharata* (including the *Bhagavad-gita*) and Ramayana; composition of *sutras*, including *Manusmriti*, *Brahma-sutra*
490–410	Life of the Buddha according to recent research
200–200 CE	Buddhism and Jainism widespread in India

Christian Era (CE)

100–500	Migration of Hindus to south-east Asia
300–900	Composition of *Puranas*
400–	Spread of Vaishnavism; beginnings of Tantrism
500–	*Devi-mahatmya* composed; spread of Shaktism; growth of temple cult and use of iconography
500–950	Flourishing of south Indian *bhakti* poetry
600–1000	Brahminical revival; decline of Buddhism in India
700–1100	Development of *Shaiva* theology
788–820	Life of Shankara
1000–	Muslim incursions into north-west India
1017–1137	Life of Ramanuja

1197–1276	Life of Madhva
1211–1526	Delhi Sultanate
c.1420	Life of Mirabai
1440–1518	Life of Kabir
c.1469	Birth of Guru Nanak, the first of the Sikh gurus
1485–1533	Life of Chaitanya
1498	Portuguese arrival in south India (Vasco da Gama)
1526–1757	Mughal rule in India
1650	British East India Company established in Bengal
1757	Victory of Clive at the Battle of Plassey
1772	Warren Hastings made Governor-General
1772–1833	Life of Ram Mohan Roy
1774	Asiatic Society founded by William Jones
1775	Translation of *Bhagavad-gita* by Charles Wilkins
1813	Missionary activity in India legalized by British Government
1820s	Growth of Swaminarayan movement
1824–83	Life of Dayananda Saraswati
1828	Brahmo Samaj formed
1829	Prohibition of *sati*
1836–86	Life of Ramakrishna
1838–	Beginning of indenture system in which Indian labourers were transported to the Caribbean, Fiji, and Mauritius
1858–1922	Life of Pandita Ramabai
1863–1902	Life of Vivekananda
1869–1948	Life of Mohandas Gandhi
1875	Arya Samaj formed; Theosophical Society formed in New York
1879–1926	Life of Sarojini Naidu
1885	Founding of Indian National Congress
1886	Ramakrishna Order formed (Ramakrishna Mission founded in 1897)
1891–1956	Life of Dr B. R. Ambedkar

1893	World Parliament of Religions, Chicago
1894	First Vedanta Society founded in New York
1896–1982	Life of Anandamayi Ma
1917	Women's India Association formed
1930	Salt march, led by Gandhi
1947	Partition of India and Indian independence
c.1950–	Migration of Hindus to West for work
1950	Constitution of India accepted
1954	Sarada Devi Math and Mission formed
1955	Untouchability Offences Act
1961	Dowry Prohibition Act
1966	Founding of the International Society for Krishna Consciousness
1992	Destruction of Babri mosque in Ayodhya by Hindu extremists
1997	K. R. Narayanan, a *dalit*, elected President of India

Glossary

Many of the scriptures of Hinduism were composed in Sanskrit (though some later ones were written in Tamil, Hindi, and other regional languages) and the words used in this book and listed below are mostly Sanskrit terms. In Sanskrit there are long and short vowel sounds, several s/sh sounds and a number of different sounds for *t* and *d* produced by placing the tongue behind the teeth or at the top of the mouth. If you would like to know more about how to pronounce these words, you might look in *Teach Yourself Sanskrit* or in a dictionary of Sanskrit. Throughout this book I have used common English spellings for Sanskrit terms, but below, as well as showing the meaning of the terms that I have used repeatedly, I have shown how they are formally transliterated from the Devanagri alphabet of Sanskrit using diacritical marks.

There are numerous regional languages in India and some of the terms I have used are rendered differently in each. Different names may be used for deities and different terms for ritual practices. Additionally, in some north Indian languages, the final *a* on many words (such as *dharma* and *Ramayana*) is not pronounced: Punjabis say 'dharam'; Gujaratis say 'Ramayan'.

advaita; *advaita*	non-duality; the form of *vedanta* associated with Shankara
Aranyakas; *Āraṇyakas*	forest treatises; Vedic scriptures, precursors to the *Upanishads*

ashrama; āśrama	stage of life
atman; ātman	the self or soul
avatara; avatāra	incarnation, usually of the god Vishnu
Bhagavad-gita; Bhagavād-gītā	the 'song of the Lord'; an important Hindu scripture, part of the *Mahabharata*
bhakti; bhakti	loving devotion
brahman; brahman	ultimate reality
Brahmanas; Brāhmaṇas	Vedic scriptures in which sacrifices are described
brahmin; brāhman	the priestly class or *varna*
dalit; dalit	the preferred name for those denoted as untouchable
darshana; darśana	seeing and being seen by the deity; philosophical perspective or system
Devi; Devī	the great Goddess
dharma; dharma	duty, law, teaching, order, sometimes 'religion'
Divali; Divālī	the festival of lights
Dravidian	name attributed to the indigenous people of India, as distinct from the Aryans
Durga; Durgā	a beneficent warrior goddess
dvaita; dvaita	duality; form of *vedanta* associated with Madhva
Ganesha; Gaṇeśa	the elephant-headed deity; remover of obstacles
ishvara; īśvara	Lord; powerful one
jati; jāti	caste
jnana; jñāna	knowledge
karma; karma	action
Krishna; Kṛṣṇa	a popular deity, depicted as a baby, cowherder, and charioteer; *avatara* of Vishnu
kshatriya; kṣatriya	warrior class or *varna*
linga; liṅga	a symbol associated with Shiva
Madhva; Madhva	thirteenth-century philosopher

Mahabharata; *Mahābhārata*	a popular epic text and source of many stories about *dharma*
mandir; maṇḍir	a temple
mantra; mantra	a verbal formula or sound which is full of power
Manusmriti; Manusmṛti	(also *Laws of Manu*) a religio-legal text describing duties of different social groups
murti; mūrti	an icon of a deity
puja; pūjā	worship in which offerings are made to a deity
Purana; Pṛāṇa	ancient; mythological and genealogical texts containing stories of gods and goddesses
Radha; Radhā	the consort of Krishna
Rama; Rāma	a popular deity beloved as king of Ayodhya; an *avatara* of Vishnu
Ramanuja; Rāmānuja	an eleventh-century philosopher
Ramayana; Rāmāyaṇa	the popular epic telling the story of Rama, Sita, and Lakshmana, of which there are many versions
Rig Veda; Ṛg Veda	the earliest Vedic text, containing hymns to the deities
rishi; ṛṣi	a sage
sampradaya; *saṁpradāya*	tradition; lineage through which teachings are handed down
samsara; saṁsāra	the cycle of birth, death, and re-birth; the world
sannyasa; saṅnyāsa	renunciation; the final stage of life; also *sannyasi*, one who has renounced the world
sati; satī	a virtuous wife; wife who burns on the funeral pyre of her husband
Shaiva; Śaiva	a follower of Shiva
Shakta; Śākta	a follower of the Goddess
shakti; śakti	divine power or energy personified as female; a name for the Goddess

Shankara; Śaṅkara	a ninth-century philosopher
Shankara-acharya; Śaṅkarācārya	a spiritual leader of the Order of Shankara
Shiva; Śiva	a major deity frequently depicted as an ascetic; auspicious one, also associated with destruction
shruti; śrūti	revealed; those early scriptures held to be revealed to *rishis* or sages
shudra; śūdra	artisan class or *varna*
Sita; Sītā	the consort of Rama, often described as the perfect wife
smriti; smṛti	remembered; those scriptures held to be remembered and handed down by tradition
sutra; sūtra	thread; an aphoristic text
Upanishad; Upaniṣad	sitting near a teacher; secret doctrine; those early scriptures in which sages enquired about the nature of ultimate reality and the self
Vaishnava; Vaiṣṇava	a follower of Vishnu
varna; varna	social class or estate
varna-ashrama-dharma; varnāśramadharma	duties according to one's social position and stage of life
Veda; Veda	knowledge; earliest Hindu scriptures, associated with the Aryans
vedanta; vedānta	the 'end of the *Veda*'; a philosophical system exploring the nature of *brahman*
vishishta; viśiṣṭa	qualified non-duality; the form of *vedanta* associated with Ramanuja
Vishnu; Viṣṇu	one who pervades everything; a major deity who maintains all; source of *avataras*
yajna; yajña	sacrifice; Vedic ritual practice in which offerings were made to the deities, often in a fire
yoga; yoga	yoking; focusing or concentrating; discipline; a system for attaining liberation.

12. *Sati* handprints: A memorial to women immolated on the funeral pyres of their husbands

Vivekananda's Achievements

1880s	Member of the Brahmo Samaj
1881	Met Ramakrishna
1886	Death of Ramakrishna; Ramakrishna Order established
1886–92	Travelled as a *sannyasi* of the Ramakrishna Order. Decisive insights at Cape Comorin
1893	Attended the World Parliament of Religions in Chicago
1893–6	Lecture tour of US and brief visit to England. (Main topics of lectures: Hinduism, especially *advaita vedanta*; East–West understanding; Indian social conditions)
1894	First Vedanta Society founded in New York
1896	Returned to India
1897	Ramakrishna Mission founded in India. Periodicals started for the dissemination of Ramakrishna's teachings
1899	Brief return to America
1902	Death of Vivekananda

The Legacy of Sarada Devi

A religious organization for women – the Ramakrishna Sarada Math and Mission – was formally established in 1954 in her name. Now also active in South Africa and Australia, it has some twenty branches in India at which women may study and live. It offers initiation to women according to vows endorsed by the orthodox *Shankara-acharya* tradition. It is one of only a few movements which enable women to renounce the world and become *sannyasinis*.

priest of the goddess Kali in the Dakshineshwara temple near Calcutta. He developed a deep relationship with the great Mother, whom he later saw present in his young wife, Sarada. He also embarked on an inner journey in which he learnt Tantric disciplines, experienced the oneness of the *advaita* vision, enjoyed love of Krishna, and explored Christian and Muslim spirituality. His profound insights and mystical behaviour impressed many people, particularly a young British-educated sceptic, Narendranath Datta (1863–1902). Later taking the name Vivekananda, it was this devotee who was to give ideological and institutional shape to his guru's vision. However, as an embodiment of the goddess, it was Sarada Devi who was to provide a spiritual focus for many of her husband's devotees.

From India to the West and Back Again

Vivekananda's chief contribution was in presenting contemporary Hindu teachings to the West, for the West. In fact, the twentieth-century Western understanding of Hinduism before the 1970s was formed largely by Vivekananda and reflected the monistic vision he referred to simply as 'Vedanta'. Vedanta Societies grew up in a number of American cities, drawing in many people disillusioned with Christianity and keen to experiment with new philosophical ideas.

When Vivekananda arrived in the West, many Americans were ready for his message. In the 1840s and 1850s, several poets had expressed ideas they believed to be akin to Upanishadic teaching on *brahman*. Ralph Waldo Emerson and Henry David Thoreau, influenced by the translations of British orientalist William Jones, had published essays on Hindu scriptures in a journal called *The Dial*. Walt Whitman, in his collection *Leaves of Grass*, had poetically expressed a philosophy which some had said was similar to Krishna's teaching in the *Bhagavad-gita*. The 'transcendentalist' poets were typical of many of those of a romantic disposition who viewed India and her religion from afar. They imagined the East to be everything the West was not: mystical,

The 'Pizza Effect'

The pizza, originally a type of plain bread, went with Italian migrants to America in the nineteenth century. There it developed into what we know today: flat bread topped with tomatoes, cheese, and anything else that might take the eater's fancy. Successful Italians returning to Italy to visit their families took with them the new-look pizza, which was then taken up in the homeland before being exported elsewhere as genuinely Italian. The export of an item, idea, or symbol, its cultural transformation, subsequent re-importation, and impact is referred to by the scholar Agehananda Bharati as 'the pizza effect'.

mythical, ritualistic, symbolic; not materialistic, rational, or scientific. They were spiritual seekers, as were the two people who later formed the Theosophical Society in New York in 1875. Madame Helena Blavatsky and Colonel H. S. Olcott began a movement with occult leanings and an interest in Hindu and Buddhist thought – particularly the ideas of *karma* and reincarnation. The Theosophical Society remained popular in the West, but also took its message eastward, settling outside Madras in 1882. Its exponents, particularly an English woman named Annie Besant (who later became leader of the Indian National Congress), preached the wonders of Hinduism, defending it against missionary criticism and evoking pride in their heritage among Indian Hindus. With Vivekananda and the Theosophical Society we see how ideas about Hinduism, fermented in the West, returned to India only to influence Hindus there. Scholars of neo-Hinduism have referred to this process as the 'pizza effect'.

Probably the clearest example of this can be seen with Mohandas K. Gandhi (1869–1948). A Gujarati Hindu nurtured in Vaishnavism and exposed to the Jain ideas of the region of his birth, Gandhi went to

Further Reading

Chapter 1

An excellent resource for the study of Hinduism will be the forthcoming eighteen-volume *Encyclopedia of Hinduism and Indic Religions,* a project of the India Heritage Research Foundation. Useful current articles include 'Hinduism' by Alf Hiltebeitel in the *Encyclopedia of Religion* (ed. Mircea Eliade, London and New York: Macmillan, 1987), vol. vi, 633–60, and 'Hinduism' by Simon Weightman in *A New Handbook of Living Religions* (ed. John Hinnells, Oxford: Blackwell, 1997). A periodical with a focus on Hinduism is the *International Journal of Hindu Studies* (Internet address: http://www.clas.ufl.edu/users/gthursby/ijhs/).

Introductory books by 'insiders': Nirad Chaudhuri, *Hinduism: A Religion to Live By* (Oxford: Oxford University Press, 1979); T. N. Madan (ed.), *Religion in India* (Oxford and Delhi: Oxford University Press, 1991); Anantanand Rambachan, *The Hindu Vision* (Delhi: Motilal Banarsidass, 1992); K. M. Sen, *Hinduism* (Harmondsworth: Penguin, 1961); Arvind Sharma, *Hinduism for Our Times* (Oxford and Delhi: Oxford University Press, 1996).

Recent introductions by 'outsiders': Gavin Flood, *An Introduction to Hinduism* (Cambridge: Cambridge University Press, 1996); Klaus Klostermaier, *A Survey of Hinduism* (New York: State University of New York Press, 1989).

Two useful books introducing aspects of the debate on early India: Romila Thapar, *Interpreting Early India* (Oxford and Delhi: Oxford University Press, 1992); Asko Parpola, *Deciphering the Indus Script* (Cambridge: Cambridge University Press, 1994).

Chapter 2

Novels and stories by Hindus are invaluable as a source of information about Hinduism and Hindu society. In addition to *Gods, Demons and Others* and *The Guide* by R. K. Narayan, there are many others by authors including Mulk Raj Anand, Kamala Markandaya, U. R. Anantha Murthy, Anita Desai, and Gita Mehta.

Books on revelation and tradition: A. L. Basham, *The Origins and Development of Classical Hinduism* (Boston: Beacon, 1989); T. J. Hopkins, *The Hindu Religious Tradition* (Encino, CA: Dickenson, 1971); K. Sivaraman (ed.), *Hindu Spirituality: Vedas Through Vedanta* (New York: Crossroad, 1989) – this is also useful for Chapter 3; Brian K. Smith, *Reflections on Resemblance, Ritual, and Religion* (New York and Oxford: Oxford University Press, 1989); M. Stutley and J. Stutley, *A Dictionary of Hinduism: Its Mythology, Folklore and Development, 1500 BC–AD 1500* (London: Routledge and Kegan Paul, 1977).

Chapter 3

Introductions to Indian philosophy: M. Hiriyanna, *Outlines of Indian Philosophy* (London: George Allen and Unwin, 1958); Ninian Smart, *Doctrine and Argument in Indian Philosophy* (London: Allen and Unwin, 1964). Selected verses by Shankara, Ramanuja, and Madhva: Sarvepalli Radhakrishnan and Charles A. Moore (eds.), *A Sourcebook in Indian Philosophy* (Princeton: Princeton University Press, 1967).

Translations of other Hindu scriptures: Wendy Doniger O'Flaherty (ed.), *Textual Sources for the Study of Hinduism* (Manchester: Manchester University Press, 1988); Ainslee T. Embree (ed.), *Sources of Indian Tradition*, vol. i, 2nd edn. (New York: Columbia University Press, 1988).

For further discussion on *karma* and *yoga*, see Rambachan, *The Hindu Vision*, Sharma, *Hinduism for Our Times*, Flood, *An Introduction to Hinduism*, and Klostermaier, *A Survey of Hinduism*.

Chapter 4

Retellings in English of stories of the gods and goddesses: Amar Chitra Katha, *Rama*, *Tales of the Mother Goddess*, *Mahabharata* (all India Book House); C. Rajagopalachari, *Ramayana* (Bombay: Bharatiya Vidya Bhavan, 1962); Wendy Doniger O'Flaherty, *Hindu Myths* (Harmondsworth: Penguin, 1975); Serinity Young (ed.), *An Anthology of Sacred Texts by and about Women* (London: Pandora, 1993).

Rama, Sita, and the Devi in contemporary Hinduism: John Stratton Hawley and Donna Marie Wulff (eds), *Devi: Goddesses of India* (Berkeley: University of California Press, 1996); Jacqueline Suthren Hurst, *Sita's Story* (Norwich: Chansitor Publications, 1997); Paula Richman (ed.), *Many Ramayanas: The Diversity of a Narrative Tradition in South Asia* (Berkeley: University of California Press, 1991); Mark Tully, *No Full Stops in India*, Chapter 4: 'The Rewriting of the *Ramayan*' (London: Penguin Books, 1991).

On the place of the *Ramayana* in Hindu nationalism: Peter van der Veer, *Religious Nationalism: Hindus and Muslims in India* (Berkeley: University of California Press, 1994).

Chapter 5

Most general books, such as those by Rambachan *The Hindu Vision*, Flood, *An Introduction to Hinduism*, and Klostermaier, *A Survey of Hinduism*, contain accounts of Hindu worship, including *puja* and pilgrimage. See also Christopher Fuller, *The Camphor Flame: Popular Hinduism and Society in India* (Princeton: Princeton University Press, 1992).

The other books listed here are excellent for gaining an understanding of the way the divine is perceived and expressed in Hindu iconography and architecture: Diana Eck, *Darsan: Seeing the Divine Image in India* (Chambersburg, PA: Anima, 1981); George Michell, *The Hindu Temple: An Introduction to its Meaning and Forms* (Chicago and London: Chicago University Press, 1988); Alistair Shearer, *The Hindu Vision: Forms of the Formless* (London: Thames and Hudson, 1993).

Chapter 6

Examples of *bhakti* poetry can be found in the books of readings by Embree *(Sources of Indian Tradition)* and O'Flaherty *(Textual Sources for the Study of Hinduism)*. Orientalist accounts of Hinduism are presented in P. J. Marshall, *The British Discovery of Hinduism in the Eighteenth Century* (Cambridge: Cambridge University Press, 1970). The lectures and writings of neo-Hindu reformers are quoted extensively in Glyn Richards, *A Sourcebook of Modern Hinduism* (London: Curzon Press, 1985).

For discussions of American transcendentalism in the nineteenth century with reference to India, see Arthur Christy, *The Orient in American Transcendentalism* (New York: Columbia University Press, 1932) and Carl T. Jackson, *The Oriental Religions and American Thought: Nineteenth-century Explorations* (Westport, CT: Greenwood Press, 1971).

For the history of the period, see H. Kulke and D. Rothermund, *A History of India* (London and New York: Routledge, 1990), and for religious movements and personalities, see Flood, *An Introduction to Hinduism*, for a brief account. A useful book on *sati* is the one edited by J. S. Hawley (ed.), *Sati, the Blessing and the Curse: The Burning of Wives in India* (New York and Oxford: Oxford University Press, 1994). See also 'The Deorala Sati' in Tully, ibid. A useful introduction to Gandhi is provided by Bhikhu Parekh's *Gandhi* (Oxford: Oxford University Press, 1997).

Chapter 7

On women: Kishwar, Madhu, and Ruth Vanita (eds.), *In Search of*

Answers: Indian Women's Voices from Manushi (London: Zed Books, 1984, reprinted New Delhi: Horizon India Books, 1991); Radha Kumar, *The History of Doing: An Illustrated Account of Movements for Women's Rights and Feminism in India, 1800–1990* (New Delhi: Kali for Women, 1993); Julia Leslie (ed.), *Roles and Rituals for Hindu Women* (London: Pinter Press, 1991); Sara S. Mitter, *Dharma's Daughters* (New Brunswick NJ: Rutgers University Press, 1991); Susie Tharu and K. Lalita (eds), *Women Writing in India, 600 BC to the Early Twentieth Century* (London: Pandora Press, 1991).

On *dalits*: Barbara R. Joshi (ed.), *Untouchable: Voices of the Dalit Liberation Movement* (London: Zed Books, 1984); Mark Juergensmeyer, *Religion as Social Vision: The Movement Against Untouchability* (Berkeley: University of California Press, 1982); Dilip Hiro, *The Untouchables of India*, Report no. 26 (Minority Rights Group, 1975). See also 'Ram Chander's Story' in Tully, *No Full Stops in India*.

Chapter 8

Books on Hindus and Hinduism beyond India: Richard Burghart (ed.), *Hinduism in Great Britain: The Perpetuation of Religion in an Alien Cultural Milieu* (London: Tavistock, 1987); John Y. Fenton, *Transplanting Religious Traditions: Asian Indians in America* (New York: Praeger, 1988); Robert Jackson and Eleanor Nesbitt, *Hindu Children in Britain* (Stoke-on-Trent: Trentham Books, 1993); Hugh Tinker, *The Banyan Tree: Overseas Emigrants from India, Pakistan, and Bangladesh* (Oxford: Oxford University Press, 1977); Steven Vertovec, *Hindu Trinidad: Religion, Ethnicity and Socio-economic Change* (London: Macmillan Caribbean, 1992); Raymond Brady Williams (ed.), *A Sacred Thread: Modern Transmission of Hindu Traditions in India and Abroad* (Chambersburg, PA: Anima, 1992).

Internet address of *Hinduism Today*:
http://www.HinduismToday.kauai.hi.us/ashram/htoday.

North American Hindu organizations are listed on the following web site: http://www.hindunet.org/

Chapter 9

The general books and articles referred to for Chapter 1 all contain discussions of the meaning of 'Hinduism'. An additional book presenting a range of contemporary perspectives is *Hinduism Reconsidered* edited by G. D. Sontheimer and H. Kulke (Delhi: Manohar, 1991).

References

Chapter 1

Nirad Chaudhuri, *Hinduism: A Religion to Live By* (Oxford: Oxford University Press, 1979), 311–29.

Chapter 2

R. K. Narayan, *Gods, Demons and Others* (London: Mandarin, 1990), 2–4; *Rig Veda* 1.1 in Wendy Doniger O'Flaherty, *Textual Sources for the Study of Hinduism* (Manchester: Manchester University Press, 1988), 6; *Manusmriti* 2.11 in Wendy Doniger O'Flaherty (ed.), *The Laws of Manu – The Laws of Manu is another name for the Manusmriti –* (Harmondsworth: Penguin, 1991); Brian K. Smith, *Reflections on Resemblance, Ritual, and Religion* (New York and Oxford: Oxford University Press, 1989), 13–17; *Rig Veda* 10.90 in Embree, *Sources of Indian Tradition*, 17–19; R. K. Narayan, *The Guide* (London: Mandarin, 1990).

Chapter 3

The Internet address for *Hinduism Today* is: http://www.HinduismToday. kauai.hi.us/ashram/htoday.html. *Upanisads* (tr. Patrick Olivelle, Oxford: Oxford University Press, 1996), 154–5; *The Complete Works of Vivekananda*, vol. viii (Calcutta: Advaita Ashrama, 1970), 101; *The Bhagavad Gita* 2.24 (tr. W. J. Johnson, Oxford: Oxford University Press, 1994), 9; *The Bhagavad Gita* 3.4, Johnson, 15; *The Bhagavad Gita* on practice of *yogin*: Johnson, 28; Patanjali on *yoga sutra*: Vivian

Worthington, *A History of Yoga* (London: Arkana, 1989), 69–78; Bal
Gangadhar Tilak, *Gita Rahasya* (Poona, 1935); Mahatma Gandhi on *karma
yoga*: Mahadev Desai, *The Gita According to Gandhi* (Ahmedabad:
Navajivan, 1946); Sharma, *Hinduism for Our Times* (Oxford and Delhi:
Oxford University Press, 1996), 36–46; *The Bhagavad Gita*, Johnson, 7–13;
Sharma, *Hinduism for Our Times*, 42.

Chapter 4

Madhur Jaffrey, *Seasons of Splendour: Tales, Myths and Legends of India*
(London: Pavilion Books, 1985), 8; Debjani Chatterjee, *I was that Woman*
(Frome: Hippopotamus Press, 1989), 23–4.

Chapter 5

Pierre Martin in P. J. Marshall, *The British Discovery of Hinduism in the
Eighteenth Century* (Cambridge: Cambridge University Press, 1970), 21;
Henry Martyn in George Smith, *The Life of Henry Martin* (London, 1892),
163; *Upanisads*, Olivelle, 46.

Chapter 6

Kabir, 'Warnings' (tr. Daniel Gold), in O'Flaherty, *Textual Sources*, 140–1;
Kabir, 'The World is Mad' (tr. Linda Hess and Sukdev Singh), in Ainslee T.
Embree, *Sources of Indian Tradition*, vol. i, 2nd edn. (New York: Columbia
University Press, 1988), 375; Warren Hastings in Marshall, *The British
Discovery of Hinduism in the Eighteenth Century*, 189; Abbé Dubois, *Hindu
Manners, Customs, and Ceremonies*, 3rd edn. (Oxford: Clarendon Press,
1906), 8; Walt Whitman, *Leaves of Grass* (Oxford: Oxford University
Press, 1990); Agehananda Bharati, 'The Hindu Renaissance and its
Apologetic Patterns', *Journal of Asian Studies* (29, 1970), 273.

Chapter 7

Chandalas as 'dog-cookers' in *The Laws of Manu* 10.108, O'Flaherty; high
caste women in *The Laws of Manu* 5.146–69, O'Flaherty; Sarojini Naidu in
Manohar Kaur, *Role of Women in the Freedom Movement, 1857–1947*
(Delhi: Sterling, 1968), 111; women's prayer in Laxmi G. Tiwari, *A

Splendour of Worship: Women's Fasts, Rituals, Stories and Art (Delhi: Manohar, 1991), 8; B. K. Ambedkar (tr. Vasant W. Moon) in Barbara R. Joshi (ed.), *Untouchable: Voices of the Dalit Liberation Movement* (London: Zed Books, 1984), 30–1; Neerav Patel, 'Burning at Both the Ends', in Joshi, *Untouchable*, 42.

Chapter 8
Richard Burghart (ed.), *Hinduism in Great Britain: The Perpetuation of Religion in an Alien Cultural Milieu* (London: Tavistock, 1987), 1–2; David Barrett (ed.), *World Christian Encyclopedia* (Oxford: Oxford University Press, 1982), *passim*.

Chapter 9
Sarvepalli Radhakrishnan, *The Hindu View of Life* (London: Mandala, 1988), 55.

Index

Page numbers in italics refer to
pictures or maps

Hinhuism